The Seventh Circle In Bible Prophecy

YHVH BLESS YOU AND PAT,

Wayne L. Atchison

The Seventh Circle In Bible Prophecy

Astronomy And The Prophetic Timelines Of The Bible

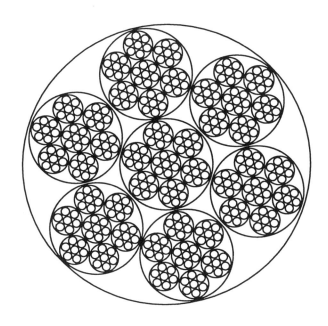

Christian Technical Notes
By
Wayne L. Atchison

VANTAGE PRESS
New York

FIRST EDITION

Copyright © 1996 by Wayne L. Atchison

Published by Vantage Press, Inc.
516 West 34th Street, New York, New York 10001

Manufactured in the United States of America
ISBN: 0-533-11872-7

Library of Congress Catalog Card No.: 96-90067

0 9 8 7 6 5 4 3 2 1

The Seventh Circle In Bible Prophecy

1.0   Introduction

From the moment of birth people are told things which are not true. From youth people are taught fairy tales, monster movies, cartoons, super heroes, Santa Claus, and Easter bunny-eggs. It is presumed that during school children are taught the truth about reading, writing, and arithmetic. However, everyone is aware that the school curriculum is no match for the higher impact commercials of the modern mass media which capitalize on the fairy tales to make money. The reality is that much of what is presented by today's mass media is blatantly not true.

One of life's bottom lines is that every person ever born inherently knows nothing external to themselves, except what they have been told by someone else. As babies people may discover their own toes, but as they grow older someone else has to teach them how to use socks and shoes, and eventually how to interpret everything else around them. Even knowledge which some people consider to be self taught or newly discovered is still knowledge directly derived or interpreted from what they had been previously taught by someone else.

This puts every person into a very vulnerable position. If what they were told is in fact not true, then they would have no way of knowing about the error, unless they just happen to listen to someone tell them differently. Throughout history it has been demonstrated that people will believe whatever they are told, as long as the truth is effectively hidden or ridiculed. For example, the Nazi war propaganda during World War II provides numerous examples of how an authority may broadcast blatant lies to the public and how the public will eventually believe those lies to be the truth. It is well understood that our modern mass media uses many of the same proven techniques to persuade people to like and buy whatever they are selling. In advertising what you tell people about the product is much more important than the truth.

Often the untruth is taken so much for granted that the truth is no longer even mentioned or recognized. As one modern example, the lending of money and the subsequent charging of interest on loans was, for most of American history, considered to be usury. Usury was not allowed and was against the banking laws. However, starting with the Civil War the usury laws have been slowly eroded by Congress. First the term "usury" was redefined from meaning: "paying interest on money based solely upon the passage of time", to meaning: "paying excessive interest on money". Later the amount considered to be "excessive interest" was incrementally increased. Even so, as recently as 1970 two-thirds of the states still had separate usury laws on the books.[1] In the early 1980's it was still possible to have some home loans declared by the courts to be illegal, based upon their violation of the still standing usury laws on the books in

---

[1]   "Encyclopedia Britanica, Inc." Copyright 1982, "Usury", Vol. 4, pages 801-803. "Loaning of Money", Vol. 4, page 993. "The Historical Development of Consumer Credit In Industrialized Countries", Vol. 5, page 99.

some states. However, just ten years later, our modern culture is so immersed into the idea that they must pay interest on loans that the concept of this practice once being forbidden by the courts and the Bible is no longer mentioned, not even by the churches. People are taught that paying interest on loans is absolutely normal. To most it now seems ridiculous to mention that this practice was once forbidden by law and is actually a violation of Biblical principles.

Such is the situation with the subjects of astronomy and modern arithmetic. Today most people do not know that there is a huge difference between astronomy and astrology. Children are taught about astrology and learn each other's signs as early as elementary school. Every entertainment media from cartoons to the newspapers consistently associate astrology with the Zodiac and its twelve signs. Movies consistently portray ancient sky watchers as astrologers practicing their fortune telling and magic. This association is now so pervasive that most people take for granted that the ancient astronomers were just astrologers performing their mystical science.

Similarly, children are taught modern arithmetic in school. Everyone is taught how to count from one to infinity. But very few are told that historically there have been other ways to perform arithmetic using different methods of counting. For example, it is rarely mentioned that there is a difference between counting numbers and counting time. Most people are totally convinced that what they were taught in school, about how to count, is the only correct way there is to count.

Presenting information which contradicts the modern illusions about astrology and arithmetic seems contrary to the most fundamental precepts learned in elementary school. It is not easy to unlearn fundamental concepts which were ingrained from childhood. But nevertheless, what is being taught in the schools and by the mass media about these two subjects is not the truth.

Perhaps the most serious untruth being taught today is that there is no Creator of the universe. Most people are taught that everything that exists is merely a result of random chance. What is taught is that the cosmos obeys the laws of physics, but has no overall organization or design. It is understood that a universe that exists without any specific organization no longer implies an intelligence behind its design.

However, imagine the significance if it were discovered that the heavens revealed a mathematically ordered relationship that is directly tied to the prophecies in the Bible. Imagine if that relationship is so strong, that there could be no possibility of the relationship occurring by random chance or by human wit. Such a discovery would give clear evidence that there is a Creator, and that the Bible's prophecies are indeed messages given to mankind by the Creator.

The truth is that the ancient science of astronomy is the studying, discovering, and recording of the Creator's handiwork in the heavens. It is this study of the heavens which provides the mathematical basis for geometry, the method for counting the passage of time, and the understanding of the prophetic timelines specified in the Bible. There is a direct relationship between the mathematical order found in the heavens and the prophecies in the Bible.

Prerequisite to understanding this relationship is to understand what the difference is between astronomy and astrology, and how to count time instead of counting numbers.

2.0   The Modern Method Of Counting Numbers

It is understood that the reader has been taught how to count. The difficulty is not in knowing how to count. The difficulty is that everyone is taught to count in a very specific manner using a very modern counting metaphor. Modern arithmetic is performed by imagining that there exists something known as "negative numbers", then something known as "zero" (nothing), and then comes "positive numbers". This concept of doing arithmetic with "a zero" is a relatively new invention of men, and it has some major problems.

For example, dividing a value by zero is said to be "undefined". It seems inconceivable that a modern scientific metaphor would leave something as "undefined". Yet the truth is that dividing a value by zero breaks the modern mathematical metaphor.

The theorem is that:

$$A \div B = Y, \text{ because } Y \times B = A$$

For example:

$$6 \div 2 = 3, \text{ because } 3 \times 2 = 6$$

But using the same theorem with the value of zero for 'B':

$$6 \div 0 = Y, \text{ because } Y \times 0 = 6 \quad \text{is invalid.}$$

There is no value for 'Y' which when multiplied by zero will equal six. The theorem is broken when the denominator is zero.

The amount of damage this one example of a broken metaphor has caused the computer industry has been enormous. The number of times that computer programs have stopped execution as they encountered the infamous "divide by zero arithmetic error" cannot be imagined. However, the concept of a "variable" being zero is so fundamental in computer mathematics that some modern computer languages are now providing the option to compute the result of dividing a value by zero to be infinity, and is not considered an error.

The root of the problem with the modern concept of doing arithmetic with "a zero" is that the concept of "nothing" is much more complicated than just the single digit of '0' can represent. There are different kinds of "nothing". There are:

- nothing as in "does not exist"
- nothing as in "empty"
- nothing as in "not started yet"
- nothing as in "too small"
- nothing as in "no difference"
- nothing as in "unknown"
- nothing as in "inapplicable"

What is most important to notice about modern arithmetic is how the count is always performed assuming a zero starting point. The count starts at one integer (like zero) and then progresses away from that starting integer in the direction of infinity. Regardless of which numerical value the count is at, when the counting begins again that integer is treated like a zero, and the count progresses away from it with the first increment to the next integer.

For example, if the count is at five and two more are counted, then the count must thereafter be at (five plus two) seven as follows:

| Five | 5 | 6 | 7 |
| Plus Two | 0 | 1 | 2 |

The five is treated like a zero and the counting progresses away from it towards seven. Counting another two is done the same way. This time the seven is treated like it were a zero, two more are counted, resulting in nine as follows:

Seven	7	8	9
Plus Two	0	1	2

In modern arithmetic the starting value is always treated as if it were a zero, and then the count moves away from it towards the next integer.

One example of a counting metaphor used in ancient times which does not use the concept of zero is called "inclusive counting". For example, in ancient times a king may have started to reign at the age of twenty. After five years of reign the king would be said to be twenty four years old as follows:

Age:	20	21	22	23	24
Reign:	1	2	3	4	5

Modern arithmetic would have computed his age to be (twenty plus five) 25 instead of 24. Also notice that using modern arithmetic to calculate in the reverse direction computes that the king only reigned (24 minus 20) four years, instead of the specified five.

The point is that when using the ancient method of inclusive counting the king's starting year is not treated like a "zero", but is counted as "one". There is no concept of a "zero" in this counting method. Much confusion has been generated by modern scholars using the wrong counting metaphor when working with ancient records.

The above explanation is a good example of why many chronology works are nearly worthless. Many such works err by using the modern counting metaphor instead of the counting metaphor employed by the ancient scribes who recorded the events.

There have been several other methods of counting used in ancient times.[2] Although modern arithmetic provides a very good metaphor to use for counting eggs, pennies, and distance, it is not the metaphor used in counting the passage of time by the ancient scholars.

3.0   The Seven Circles Method Of Counting

As the modern world turns more and more towards digital electronics, the concept of counting using circles may at

---

[2]   "Serpent In The Sky", by John Anthony West. Copyright 1993. The Theosophical Publishing House, P.O. Box 270, Wheaton, IL 60189-0270. ISBN 0-8356-0691-0. Pages 32, 43, 45, 55 - 56. Examples of other counting metaphors include using triangles within squares, triangle grids, hexagon grids, pentagram, tetractys, and the enneagram.
"The Rhind Mathematical Papyrus, An Ancient Egyptian Text", by Gay Robins & Charles Shute. Copyright 1987. British Museum Publications, Ltd. 46 Bloomsbury Street, London WC1B 3QQ. This book is devoted to describing what may only be summarized as "the Egyptian way of doing math and algebra". Even though the Egyptians used base-10, they had no zero and accomplished multiplication, division, fractions, geometry, and algebra much differently than we do today. Their methods accurately computed the correct answers, but was a different way of doing math.

first thought seem to be as strange as using analog computers. But upon considering the shapes found in nature and in astronomy, circles within circles are discovered to be a very common pattern. For example, circles within circles are seen in a diagram of our solar system, and in the ripples of water caused by the splash of a rock in a pool.

Consider the look of a natural occurring honeycomb made by bees. Looking at the honeycomb an observer may perceive much more than the hundreds of hexagon shaped cells, and begin to notice the obvious pattern of circles within circles emerging. Regular hexagons and circles are naturally related shapes and have unique properties which allow for counting very large numbers.

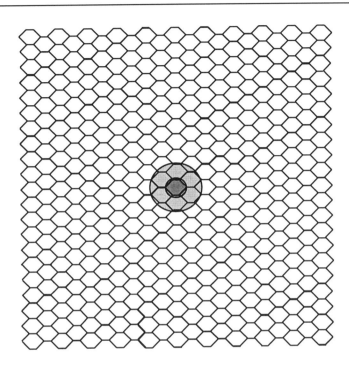

1. Lattice of Regular-Hexagons Forms Circles Within Circles

While counting the cells within a honeycomb, the task is not to count each and every cell in a linear fashion. One could use sticks to employ that method. The task is to use the cells in a manner which creates distinctive patterns that are capable of counting and representing very large numbers. The most natural and obvious distinctive pattern to use is the circle within a circle. Within this distinctive pattern the simple task is to count cells, and to progressively move outwards to form larger and larger rings of cells as the counting continues.

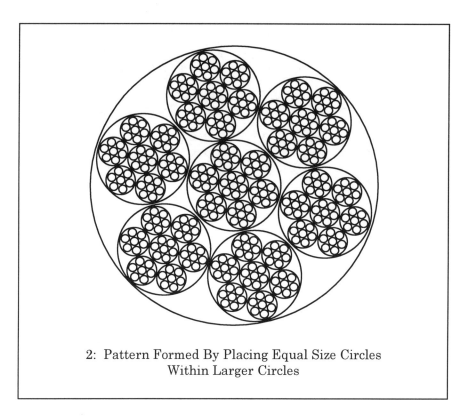

2: Pattern Formed By Placing Equal Size Circles
Within Larger Circles

Drawing six equal size circles around in a circular pattern creates something unique. The shape or form created by their pattern implies the existence of two other circles, an outer larger circle, and a seventh circle which fits right in the middle of the other six. Arranging six circles in a ring pattern implies both a seventh and an eighth circle.

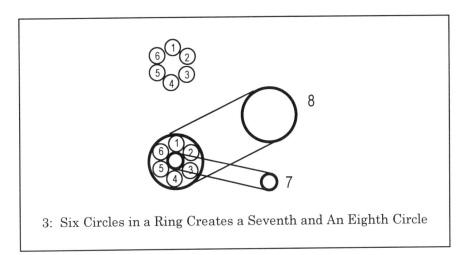

3: Six Circles in a Ring Creates a Seventh and An Eighth Circle

The larger eighth circle encapsulates the seven smaller inner circles and thereby becomes a new circle in a larger pattern. By placing six of these eighth-circles in a larger ring, a larger pattern is formed which again implies a seventh and an eighth circle.

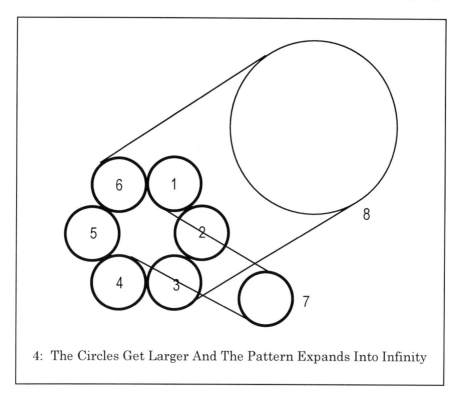

4: The Circles Get Larger And The Pattern Expands Into Infinity

The new even larger eighth circle may be used to form another ring, and so on. Thus the basic pattern formed by placing circles within circles will keep expanding with larger and larger patterns into infinity.

The process of counting by using circles within circles is not difficult. In the first-ring it is apparent that counting up to six and then seven presents no problem. Counting the eighth circle forces something else to happen first. What happens next defines the method of counting using circles.

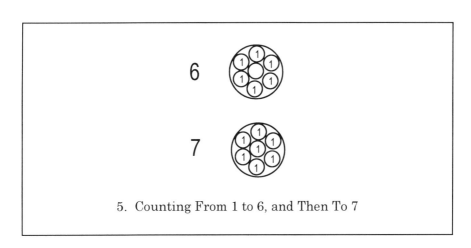

5. Counting From 1 to 6, and Then To 7

The fundamental idea not to overlook is that the first-ring of seven counted circles represents the count value of seven. Once each of the seven circles in the first-ring are counted, that ring is complete. The procedure to count the eighth circle is to first expand the pattern outward to the next larger ring of circles. After drawing six new and uncounted first-rings to form the next larger second-ring of circles, the original first-ring is marked as being completed, and a new count is begun in another circle.

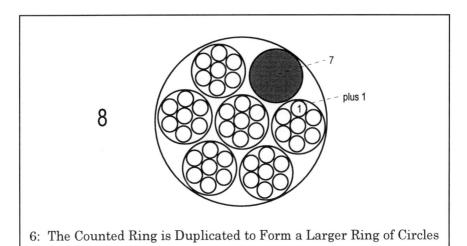

6: The Counted Ring is Duplicated to Form a Larger Ring of Circles

The simplest way of describing this procedure is that after a ring is fully counted, to count the next circle forces the pattern to expand to the next larger ring. Then the fully counted ring is marked as completed, and a different circle is selected to continue the count.

Continuing the count past eight will result in the other six newly formed first-rings to eventually become fully counted, marked as complete, and the count continued within another circle.

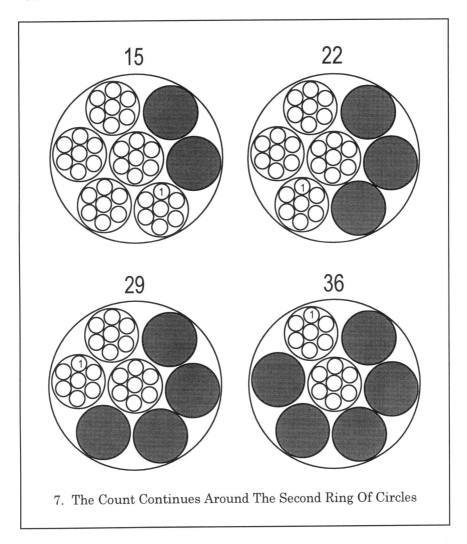

7. The Count Continues Around The Second Ring Of Circles

After all seven circles of a first-ring are counted, the "carry-over" into the next first-ring will occur at the values of 15, 22, 29, 36, and 43.

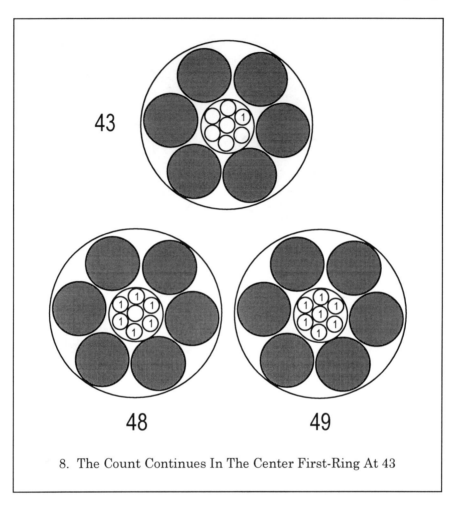

8. The Count Continues In The Center First-Ring At 43

Upon counting to 49, all circles within the second-ring will have been fully counted. To count to 50 then requires the same procedure to be followed. The pattern is expanded to the next larger ring, the fully counted ring is marked completed, and a new circle is selected to continue the count.

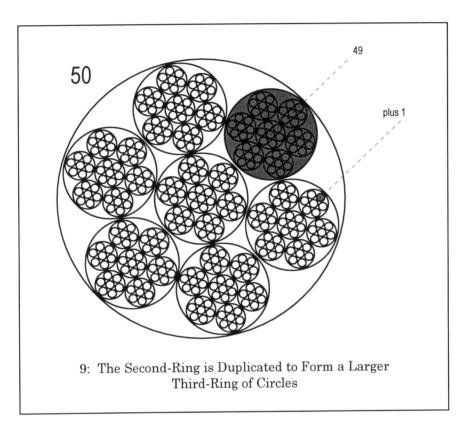

9: The Second-Ring is Duplicated to Form a Larger
Third-Ring of Circles

It is apparent that each of the six new second-rings used in forming the new larger third-ring are each capable of counting up to 49, just as the original second-ring had done before the pattern expanded. By calculation it can be determined that this new larger pattern is capable of counting up to (49 times 7 rings) 343.

When the count gets to 344, the pattern is again expanded to form the next larger fourth-ring of circles.

Within this next larger fourth-ring, each of its six new inner third-rings are capable of counting up to 343 each, resulting in the new fourth-ring pattern being capable of counting up to (343 times 7 rings) 2,401.

By extension it can be determined that counting within a pattern having ten rings deep results in a pattern capable of progressively counting from 1 through each ring as follows:

> 7 : 49 : 343 : 2,401 : 16,807 : 117,649 : 823,543 :
> 5,764,801 : 40,353,607 : 282,475,249.

This is also the same progression as 7 raised to the power of 1, 2, 3, and so forth, and in this example ending at 7 to the 10th power which is 282,475,249. The number of rings in the pattern may be expanded infinitely.

Some readers may recognize that this method of counting is actually another method of counting within the base-7 system. In modern arithmetic the base-10 system is taught, which uses numerals 0 through 9. Therefore the value '119' is (1 times 100) plus (1 times 10) plus 9. In base-7 the numerals only range from 0 through 6. The base-10 number '123' would be '234' in base-7. That is, (2 times 49) plus (3 times 7) plus 4, (98 + 21 + 4 = 123). Counting using circles within circles has each larger ring representing higher powers of 7, just as the base-7 system does. The value '123' base-10 would then be "2 circles counted, 3 circles counted, 4 circles counted".

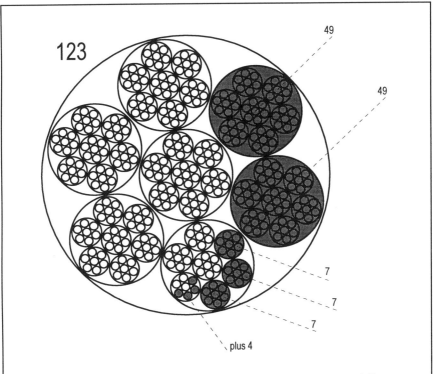

10: The Value '123' is '234' in the Seven Circles Method of Counting

3.1   Significant Numbers In The Seven Circles Method

It is very interesting to notice which numbers have significance in this different method of counting. For example, the value seven completes a ring, or makes the first-ring perfect. Nearly all cultures recognize the value seven as the value for "perfection" and "completeness".[3]

The value eight is significant in that it forces the pattern to expand and thereby starts a new larger second-ring. The value eight is most often associated with "new beginnings" and "new birth".[4]

The value 49 is reached when the second-ring is fully counted. The value 49 is called the value of "seven perfections" and "perfect consummation of time".[5]

---

[3]   "The Arithmetic Of God", by Don Kistler. Copyright 1976. The Arithmetic of God, P.O. Box 573, Kings Mountain, NC, 28086. Page 46.
"Numbers In Scripture", by E.W. Bullinger. Copyright 1981. Kregel Publications, Grand Rapids, MI 49501. ISBN 0-8254-2238-8. Page 167. In Hebrew, the word for seven is "shevah", which has the root of "to be full or satisfied, to have enough of".
"Theomatics", by Jerry Lucus. Copyright 1977. Stein and Day Publishers, Scarborough House, Briarcliff Manor, NY 10510. ISBN 0-8128-2181-5. This book is highly recommended for those readers interested in learning another discipline providing overwhelming evidence that there is a Creator and that the Bible is authored by Him. This book documents how the words used to comprise the scriptures numerically add up to very specific values and in very consistent ways. This book documents how the Bible is filled with so many consistent numerical patterns that the probability that one or more men, without being lead by a divine author, could have written the scriptures so mathematically consistent is clearly impossible.

[4]   "The Arithmetic Of God", page 48.
[5]   "The Arithmetic Of God", page 268.

Like the value of eight, the value of 50 forces the second-ring to expand, which also starts a larger pattern. In Leviticus chapter 25 the value 50 is used to count to the year of Jubilee. The Jubilee is called "the year of new beginnings" as it was decreed that in that year all debts were to be forgiven, and all lands returned back to their original owners.

The number 50 was highly prevalent in the construction of the Tabernacle of Moses. For example it was decreed that the Tabernacle include 50 loops for the curtains, with 50 taches, and that the court was to be 50 cubits wide and 100 (50 times 2) cubits long.[6]

The festive Holy Day of Pentecost also involves the counting of 50 days. More accurately, as described in Leviticus 23:16 and 25:8-12, the process is to complete the counting of seven-sevens (Sabbaths). This is the same process as counting seven circles having seven circles each. Pentecost is the next day (the first circle counted in the expanded pattern).

By extension it should follow that the values of 343 and 2,401 are also values signifying perfection as they complete the third and fourth rings. Likewise, the values 344 and 2,402 are also values signifying new beginnings

---

6   "The Interlinear Bible", by Jay P. Green, Sr. Copyright 1986. Hendrickson Publishers, Peabody, Massachusetts 01961-3473. ISBN 0-913573-25-6. Exodus 26:5-11 and 27:12-18. All Biblical references and quotes from the Bible are taken from this work, unless otherwise noted.

as they force the pattern to expand into the next larger fourth and fifth rings.

The numbers 15, 22, 29, 36, and 43 are also related to the concept of new beginnings, as they are the first count after completing a neighboring first-ring. Notice that our own calendar, passed down to us from Roman times, incorporates the basic concept of counting seven days to complete a weekly cycle (a circle), with the next weekly cycle beginning on the counts of 8, 15, 22, and 29.

SUN	MON	TUE	WED	THR	FRI	SAT
1	2	3	4	5	6	7
8	9	10	11	12	13	14
15	16	17	18	19	20	21
22	23	24	25	26	27	28
29	30	31				35

11. The Calendar Has A Seven Day Cycle With Each Week Beginning On 1, 8, 15, 22, and 29

Also of interest is that the Bible in Leviticus 23 has specified that two festive Holy Days be celebrated on the 15th day of the first and the seventh months, and that a third Holy Day be celebrated on the 22nd day of the seventh month.

3.2   The Seven Circles Method And The Jubilee

Another important effect of this method of counting is that it explains why the Biblical Jubilee years are not 50 years apart from each other, but rather they are only 49 years apart.

Many have seen this fact to be a contradiction as they use modern arithmetic to perform the count to 50. Modern arithmetic is linear, each number counts once towards the next number and progresses linearly away from the previous number on into infinity. There is no concept of a number "counting twice" or being both 50 and 1 at the same time. Therefore, using modern arithmetic and counting to the next Jubilee, which is said to be the 50th year, would result in a progression of 0, 50, 100, 150, and so forth.

However, counting using the Seven Circles Method is not necessarily a linear progression towards infinity. In this method of counting it is the 50th count which forces the expansion of the pattern and a new beginning as the counting continues in another ring. The point to notice is that the 50th circle may be thought of as being counted twice, once to expand the pattern and second to mark the first circle within a new ring.

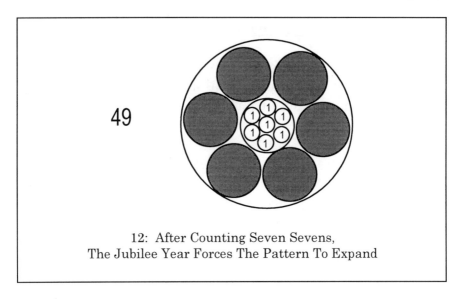

12: After Counting Seven Sevens,
The Jubilee Year Forces The Pattern To Expand

In this method of counting, celebrating the importance of the 50th year, is not actually claiming that it is an integer increment in a linear fashion counting towards infinity. Rather it is more like celebrating the expansion of the pattern and recognizing the first year of each progressive series of 49 years (the beginning of each new second-ring).

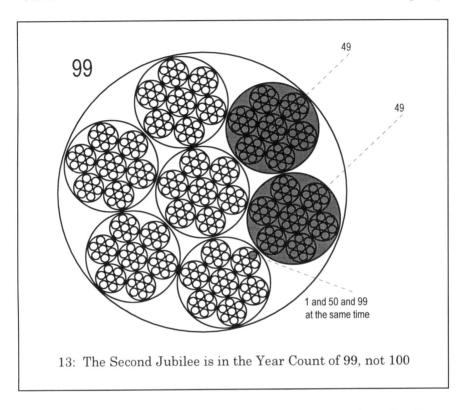

13: The Second Jubilee is in the Year Count of 99, not 100

When counting with circles the value 50 is also the first circle counted in a new ring, it is both 50 and 1 at the same time. The Jubilee celebrates the year of new beginnings after each ring of 49 years has been completed.

4.0   Units Of Measure In Geometry, And Time

Geometry is a subject that many people remember from their school days with some measure of pain. It is not the easiest subject to learn or teach. What has always been very awkward to explain is why a circle is divided into 360 parts called degrees. Why the number 360? Think about how much easier many aspects of geometry would be if a different number, like say 100, were used instead. Remember working with latitude and longitude. The coordinate system is 360 degrees, 60 minutes, and 60 seconds. Why the number 60? Where did 60 come from?

Consider the everyday clock. It has 12 hours, 60 minutes, and 60 seconds. Why the number 12? The day has 24 hours. Why the number 24? How did anyone ever decide to use these numbers when values like 10 or 20 or 100 make much better numbers for much easier calculations?

Consider other systems used for counting time. For instance the Hillel II calendar (commonly known as the Jewish Calendar) was created only about 1,650 years ago, around 350 Common Era (CE, same as A.D.). This calendar counts time in the familiar 24 hour days, but does not use minutes or seconds to split the hour out as is done today. Instead each hour is divided into 1,080 parts, where each part is about 3.333 of today's seconds. How could anyone decide that splitting an hour into 1,080 parts was the right thing to do?

What is astounding is that none of these "strange" values used for counting time and used for measuring circles are arbitrary, nor were they randomly chosen. On the contrary, each of these values are directly derived from having a knowledge of astronomy, the ecliptic, and the reason the earth has its four seasons. Nearly everything about what we know of as simple geometry comes directly from astronomy. The seemingly unlikely values of 1080, 360, 60, 24, and 12 are all related astronomically and geometrically. They are directly derived by counting time using circles. The movements in the heavens, astronomy, geometry, and counting time using circles are completely interrelated.

5.0   The Zodiac In Astronomy

The word "Zodiac" is what is called a "loaded word". Just by printing the word to be read will immediately conjure up a predisposed religious opinion about it in the reader's mind. Many have been taught that the twelve constellations of the Zodiac were derived from astrology, and therefore are icons of evil. It is because of this untruth that many retract their minds as soon as the word "Zodiac" is used in their presence. The retracted mind cannot be taught.

It is not contested that astrology is another religion, with premises that are very far apart from Judaic-Christian tenets. Being a different religion, astrology should be avoided by Christians. However, the belief that the stars of the Zodiac and the twelve constellations came from the religion of astrology is simply not true historically.

Because the subject of the Zodiac and its twelve houses will come up many times in this writing, an explanation of the word "Zodiac" and its history must be presented before proceeding.

5.1   The Zodiac, Is It Astronomy Or Astrology

It is unfortunate, but it seems that the Zodiac is always tied to astrology every time the subject is presented by the mass media.   In the newspaper, in commercials, in movies, on the radio, at county fairs, in children's books, in adult books, in art, and in modern literature, the Zodiac and astrology are associated together as being one and the same.   For this reason, to claim that they are not really associated together sounds ridiculous.   Therefore, a distinction will be made between what is taught every day within our modern society and what is historically true from ancient times.   It is true that today "everyone" is taught to associate the Zodiac with astrology.   It is also true that this teaching is in error.

What is true historically is that the religion of astrology has been practiced since before the great flood of Noah. After the flood the practice of worshipping the "Host of Heaven" was a rival religion to that of worshipping the Creator, just as it is today.

Also true is that through the science of astronomy the astrologers are enabled to promote their tenets. Astronomers do not have to practice astrology, but astrologers must rely upon the science of astronomy to practice their religion.

As will be documented in the following sections, what is not true is that the religion of astrology invented the Zodiac with its twelve constellations, nor that astrology was ever sanctioned as legitimate by those who studied astronomy. There has always been a clear distinction between astronomy as a science and astrology as a religion, especially prior to circa 1960 CE.

5.2   Astronomy Versus Astrology

One example is taken from "The Works of Josephus" in his account of the Biblical patriarch Abraham who it is said: "taught the Egyptians a more perfect science of astronomy". The following is Josephus' account of Abraham speaking to the Egyptians:

> " 'That there was but one God, the Creator of the universe; and that, as to other gods [within context this means the sun, moon, and planets], if they contributed anything to the happiness of men, that each of them afforded it only according to his [the Creator's] appointment, and not by their own power.' This his opinion was derived from the irregular phenomena that were visible both at land and sea, as well as those that happen to the sun and moon, and all the heavenly bodies, thus: 'If [said Abraham] these bodies had power of their

own, they would certainly take care of their own regular motions, but since they do not preserve such regularity, they make it plain, that in so far as they cooperate to our advantage, they do it not of their own abilities, but as they are subservient to him [the Creator] that commands them; to whom alone we ought justly to offer our honor and thanksgiving.' "[7]

Acknowledging that the writing style employed by Josephus may seem awkward, a careful reading of the above text makes several points very clear:

1) Abraham's audience believed that the motions of the sun, moon, and planets affected men, which of course is the fundamental tenet of astrology. This gives evidence that the belief in astrology existed over 1,100 years prior to the Babylonian astrologers.

2) Abraham knew about the science of astronomy which studies the Creator's handiwork by investigating the motions of the sun, moon, and planets in the heavens.

---

[7]   "The Works of Josephus", Translated by William Whiston. Copyright 1987. Hendrickson Publishers, Peabody, Massachusetts, 01961-3473. ISBN: 0-913573-86-8. Quotation from "The Antiquities Of The Jews", Chapter 7, Paragraph 1, page 38.

3) The Creator made the sun, moon, and planets. It is the Creator which preserves them, and is their commander.

4) The primary purpose behind Abraham's speech was to convince the audience to worship the Creator who commands, rather than the sun, moon, and planets which are nothing but the servants of the Creator.

5) For the readers who like historical astronomy, even at the time of Abraham, circa 1950 Before Common Era (BCE, equivalent to 1950 B.C.), the motions of the sun, moon, and planets were irregular.

From the above it is manifest that the larger issue being debated by Abraham was that the study of the motions of the sun, moon, and planets, which is astronomy, was in essence studying the works of the Creator, and that the worship of the sun, moon, and planets as gods, which is astrology, was a religion taking honor away from the Creator.

Modern education and the mass media teach that in ancient cultures knowledge of astronomy was very primitive. This portrayal of our ancestors being incapable of having accumulated any significant amount of astronomical knowledge is so ingrained into our western culture, that every time an archeologist uncovers something to the contrary, the first proposal is to either call it a "great mystery" or to suggest that it must have been accomplished by "extra-terrestrials".

This form of vain presumption is totally baseless. For example, the ancient Chinese still have preserved in their own archives astronomical data collected by observers dating back more than 4,000 years. From an article describing the Chinese "Bamboo Annals":

> "For more than 4,000 years, the Chinese have kept astonishingly accurate astronomical records, an academic and intellectual tradition that survives to this day. Beijing Observatory has already published an astounding compilation of 1.5 million words of astronomy, drawn from more than 150,000 historical texts. In historical times, Chinese astronomers duly recorded all but two of the 30 appearances of Halley's Comet. There is every reason to believe that their more ancient predecessors were just as precise. One of the earliest recorded observations by Chinese astronomers was a total eclipse of the sun that occurred on October 16, 1876 B.C.."[8]

---

[8]　　"Archaeology" Magazine, September/October 1989. "Dating By Solar Eclipses", by Brian Fagan. Copyright 1989. Archaeological Institute of America, 135 William Street, New York, NY 10038. Pages 20 - 23.
This total eclipse was verified by Mr. Fagan, and was independently verified by this author using his own commercially available astronomy software.

Also consider the Egyptian astronomers in the context of the pyramids.[9] The astronomical accuracy found within

9   "The Orion Mystery", by Robert Bauval and Adrian Gilbert. Copyright 1994. Crown Publishers, Inc., 201 East 50th Street, New York, NY 10022. ISBN 0-517-59903-1. Page 230 - 236. Modern scholars are completely in error when they suggest that the sophistication of the ancient pyramid builders was primitive. For example, one of the items found within the Great Pyramid was a bronze hook discovered in 1872, proving that the pyramid builders knew how to make bronze tools. Another item was an iron plate found in 1837, proving that they knew how to forge iron ore. These are metallurgic skills normally assigned only to "modern" cultures, yet they were used during the construction of the Great Pyramid.

"Secrets Of Lost Races, New Discoveries of Advanced Technology In Ancient Civilizations", by Rene Noorbergen. Copyright 1977. Harper & Row, Publishers, Inc. 10 East 53rd Street, New York, NY 10022. ISBN 0-06-464025-6. Pages120 - 131. This chapter describes the historical situation where many of the Egyptian pyramids were discovered by archaeologists during the nineteenth century, prior to the modern advent of the airplane. Consequently, when these archaeologist reviewed and classified the artifacts they found, they categorized many objects under the simple title of "Bird Artifacts". Later, in 1969, Dr. Kalil Messiha was cleaning out a museum's basement storage area and realized that one of the "birds" was in fact an "airplane". The artifact had been taken from a tomb near Saqqara, dated approximately 200 BCE, and was catalogued as No. 6347, Rm. 22. In 1971 the ancient artifact was analyzed and tested within wind-tunnels by a panel of experts. Their conclusion was to certify that the ancient object was indeed an actual scale model of a lager well designed aircraft.
From page 126: "More recently, several other model planes have been uncovered from other tombs and identified,

the geometry, proportions and perfect north-south and east-west alignment of the pyramids are staggering. The measurements within the Great Pyramid leave no doubt that they knew many astronomical details, including the circumference of the earth and the sidereal, solar, and anomalistic years.[10] In fact, many scholars now argue that the ancients in nearly every culture had acquired very significant astronomical knowledge, especially regarding the Chinese and Egyptian astronomer's knowledge of the precession.[11]

---

bringing the total number of Egyptian gliders to fourteen. As biologist-zoologist Ivan T. Sanderson, head of the Society for the Investigation of the Unexplained, commented, 'The concrete evidence that the ancients knew of flight was forced upon us only a few years ago. Now we have to explain it. And when we do we will have to rearrange a great many of our concepts of ancient history.' ".

The chapter also describes discoveries of ancient aircraft from other parts of the world, specifically Babylon, India, China, pre-Inca northern Columbia, and among the Polynesians.

[10]   "The Great Pyramid Decoded", by E. Raymond Capt. Copyright 1971. Artisan Sales, P.O. Box 1497 Thousand Oaks, CA 91360. Pages 64 - 65.

[11]   "The Orion Mystery", page 190.

Some object strongly to the idea that the ancients were accomplished astronomers. In their objections it is often asserted that the ancients lacked telescopes, without which they could not perform accurate astronomical observations, nor confirm that the planets revolved around the sun by noticing that Venus has phases like our own moon. To dispel this objection the following reference is included:

"Stellar Theology and Masonic Astronomy", by Robert Hewitt Brown. No Copyright notice. Kessinger Publishing Company, P.O. Box 160-C, Kila, MT 59920. ISBN 1-56459-357-6. Pages

The practice of ancient astronomers studying the movements of the objects in the heavens is a documented fact of history. The distinction between the science of astronomy and the religion of astrology has also been clearly documented by the ancient historians. As one example:

> "By the beginning of the Christian era, ... the Greek historian Strabo writes: 'In Babylon, a settlement is set apart for the local astronomers, the Chaldeans, as they are called, who are concerned mostly with astronomy; but some of them who are not approved by the others, profess to be astrologers'."[12]

Notice that even as late in history as the first century CE that the distinction between astronomy and astrology was

---

31 - 33, "What The Ancients Knew About Astronomy". This section concentrates on documenting, with quotes from historical writers and modern archaeological finds, how the ancient Babylonians, Egyptians, and later the Greeks and Romans made glass lenses specifically for optical purposes. These lenses were also used to make telescopes for use in astronomy. The documentation even describes how Nero used "glasses" to watch the fights of the gladiators.

From page 33: "It appears that, in the time of Pythagoras, 'optic glasses', contrived to increase the power of vision, were so common as not to be regarded as objects of curiosity... (Baldwin's "Prehistoric Nations", pages 178-179)."

12   "Early Man and The Cosmos", by Walker & Company, NY. Copyright 1984. Library of Congress CCN 83-42727. ISBN 0-8027-0745-9. Page 16.

well understood by Strabo and his readers. The ancient author did not have to explain to his readers the distinction between the words "astronomy" and "astrologers". Notice that the Babylonian astronomers were the ones called "Chaldeans", not the astrologers. It was the astrologers who were not approved (this means socially outcast, not greeted in public) by the astronomers.

The fact that it was the astronomers who held the "higher social position" can be deduced in that the settlement was set apart on their behalf and for their sky watching pursuits. Evidence showing that it was the astronomers who held the "higher scholastic position" can be derived from the following evidence:

> "After only a single year of collaboration, however, Strassmaier and Epping managed to demonstrate that the Babylonian scribes had predicted the motion of the moon with startling mathematical precision. ... It is certain, however, that Babylonian sky watchers was an elite activity. Only intensively trained scribes could master the five hundred basic signs of cuneiform writing; the priests and kings were illiterate, relying on the scribes to inform them of portents and predictions related to the sky. The scribes were secular officials, but their quarters were often attached to the temple. Later on, their skills seem to have been passed down among a few aristocratic families. The exclusiveness of their knowledge ensured a remarkable continuity in the keeping of records. When the Assyrian scholar - tyrant

Ashurbanipal (668 - 630 BCE) founded his great library at Nineveh, ... he took care to preserve astronomical documents from the old Babylonian Period [taken] more than a thousand years earlier [this would be back to circa 1650 BCE]."[13]

Although it may be speculation on the part of the above quoted author regarding the degree of illiteracy of the priests and kings of Babylon, it is still "certain" that the knowledge and duty of astronomical predictions about eclipses and seasons of the year and their official monthly calendar was held exclusively by a selective group of well educated scribes (scholars). The secret knowledge was kept "in the family" and passed down through the years. This same line of scholars still existed in the first century CE and were called astronomers. Also notice that the ancient records of these Babylonian astronomers dated back to circa 1650 BCE, and other sources describe data going back to 2234 BCE[14].

History is filled with examples giving evidence that astrology has always been distinguished from astronomy, and has always been considered to be an outcast practice.

---

13   "Early Man and The Cosmos", pages 11 and 12.
14   "Stellar Theology and Masonic Astronomy", "What The Ancients Knew About Astronomy". Page 32: "We are informed by Simplicius that Callisthenes, who accompanied Alexander to Babylon [circa 331 BCE], sent to Aristotle from that capital [Babylon] a series of astronomical observations, which he had found preserved there, extending back to a period of 1,903 years before Alexander's conquest of that city, or 2234 B.C."

Consider the historical account describing how all of astrologers were expelled from Rome and Italy in 139 BCE.[15] This is over a hundred years before Julius Caesar. Later in Roman history Saint Augustine (circa 354 - 430 CE) writes in his confessions:

> "The very struggle to become a Christian - to abandon pagan superstition for Christian free will - seemed to be a struggle against astrology."[16]

A more modern example of the difference between astronomy and astrology may be learned from the following:

> "It should be noted however, that when astronomers speak of Aries, they are referring to the constellation Aries, whereas when astrologers speak of Aries, they mean the sign of Aries, that is, one of the twelve areas of the zodiac that the sun takes a month to cross. There was a time, in the 2nd century BC, when signs and constellations coincided with each other; unfortunately, the precession of the equinoxes, that slippage of the

---

[15]   "The Discoverers, A History of Man's Search To Know His World And Himself", by Daniel J. Boorstin. Copyright 1983. Random House, Inc. New York, NY. ISBN 0-394-40229-4. Page 19.

[16]   "The Discoverers, A History of Man's Search To Know His World And Himself", pages 23 - 24. Describes how astrology was the "bete noire" of the Christian church fathers. They were constantly in a struggle against the contrary faith of astrology.

sun's 'path' through the stars, has played a nasty trick on astrologers: As the point at which the sun crosses the equator in the spring is progressively altered, so are the astrologer's signs. . . . For example, the sign of Aries now covers the constellation of Pisces; however, astrologers believe that the area of the sky in which the constellation of Aries used to lie, more than two thousand years ago, has retained that animal's positive virtues..."[17]

The science of astronomy is looking at the stars as being part of the Zodiac's definition, while the astrologers are pretending like the Zodiac does not move, and ignoring the fact that the stars are no longer within their signs. The main point to be noticed from the above quote is that astronomers and astrologers may be using the same words, for example: "the sun is in Aries", but the words do not mean the same thing by more than two thousand years of precession.

The modern mass media would have everyone believe that the religion of astrology was rampant during the European dark ages. This is simply not true. Consider the well known fact that the Roman Church, and later the Protestant Churches, all considered astrology to be sorcery. Those condemned of practicing sorcery were executed as witches or warlocks. There is no doubt that

---

17   "The Sky, Mystery, Magic, and Myth", by Jean-Pierre Verdet. No Copyright Notice. Abrams Discoveries, Harry N. Abrams, Inc. Publishers, New York. ISBN 0-8109-2873-6. Page 42-43.

these Church organizations held the primary social and political influence throughout this time period.

What is also manifest from history is that the Zodiac and its constellations were used extensively in the study of astronomy. Those in power well understood that using the Zodiac's signs and constellations in the science of astronomy was not the same as practicing astrology. Therefore the astronomical use of the Zodiac was approved by the religious, political, and social order during the Middle Ages. For example, the Zodiac appears for navigation purposes prominently on nearly all maps drawn during this era.

But astrology was never tolerated by the churches and was reflected in the laws of Europe. The religion of astrology was, and throughout history always has been, an underground and outcast activity. Only since circa 1960 CE has astrology been mass media blitzed into every one's daily acceptance.

5.3   Ptolemy In Western Astronomy

Historically what happened was that during the Middle Ages most of the European astronomers were taught and relied upon the writings of an astrologer named Ptolemy.[18]   Ptolemy lived and practiced astrology in

---

[18]   "Ancient Planetary Observations And The Validity Of Ephemeris Time", by Robert R. Newton. Copyright 1976. The John Hopkins University Press, Baltimore, Maryland 21218.

Alexandria Egypt circa 142 CE. In his practice of astrology Ptolemy endeavored to understand several mathematical aspects of astronomy and wrote two books, the "Syntaxis" and the "Tetrabiblos".

Unfortunately, Ptolemy's writings were among the few astronomy writings to survive into the Middle Ages through the Greek culture.[19] These writings then represented the only record of Hellenistic astronomy prior to 142 CE. However, Ptolemy's records were not exhaustive. As a result of relying upon Ptolemy, nearly all of the pre-Greek astronomy records were lost to the western European astronomers of the Middle Ages. However in modern times we have access to many pre-Greek astronomy records, as they were preserved by the astronomers in India.[20]

This reliance upon Ptolemy was created because of the political and religious forces which dramatically split the

---

ISBN 0-8018-1842-7. The following historical dissertation is primarily taken from pages 50, 58, 84, 147, 149-150, 165, 221, and 219.

[19] "The Discoverers, A History of Man's Search To Know His World And Himself", page 20: The great library at Alexandria was burnt by Julius Caesar. Many other great libraries were reduced to ashes by Christian and Islamic armies. A tremendous volume of information and data was forever lost.
"Encyclopedia Britanica, Inc.", Vol. 1, page 479, under "Alexandria": The library at Alexandria was burnt by a Christian army in 391 CE, and later burnt again by an Islamic army in 642 CE.

[20] "Ancient Planetary Observations And The Validity Of Ephemeris Time", page 219.

western and eastern world. These forces were the Roman versus Parthian empires, and later the Christian versus Islamic faiths. Due to this split, the western astronomers effectively lost access to the records and astronomy techniques taught in the astronomy academies extant in the Persian / Ottoman empire. Generally speaking, the eastern world followed the Persian astronomy and the western world followed Ptolemy's astronomy.[21]

Without adequate historical data to suggest otherwise, the western astronomers came to solely rely upon Ptolemy's astronomical calculations, techniques, and star maps. In the absence of other materials they believed that Ptolemy's writings provided the correct methods for making astronomical predictions. This reliance upon Ptolemy is the reason why western astronomy fell so far behind the astronomical methods known and practiced in the east.

The brutal fact is that Ptolemy was not a very knowledgeable astronomer. In modern times his work has been critically scrutinized. In the light of modern computers and astronomy, it is clear that Ptolemy's methods were wrong, inaccurate, and inferior to the methods known in the east. It has also been discovered that much of his work was not based upon astronomical observations. Rather he used his own calculation techniques to make predictions about observations, and then listed them as having taken place. There are other

---

[21]   "Ancient Planetary Observations And The Validity Of Ephemeris Time", page 58.

instances of outright fraud in which Ptolemy forced calculation values in order to succeed in demonstrating that his calculation techniques worked.[22]

Thus, by using Ptolemy's astronomy techniques the sophistication of western astronomy fell dramatically during the Middle Ages. However, this was not true in the eastern world. As trade between the east and west increased, so did the exchange of astronomical information. For example Pope Sylvester II (the Pope during 993 - 1003 CE) wrote extensively on astronomy but used the Arabic terms in doing so.[23]

Even though it is true that Ptolemy was an astrologer, and that his writings became the primary source for western astronomy after circa 140 CE, it is not true that most astronomers using Ptolemy's star maps and astronomical calculation techniques changed religions and engaged in the practice of astrology. From the historical accounts it may be seen that at all times and in both the Islamic and Christian cultures the science of astronomy was practiced, and the religion of astrology was forbidden.

An excellent publication which very effectively defends astronomy and scientifically disproves astrology is a

22   "Ancient Planetary Observations And The Validity Of Ephemeris Time", pages 149-150.
23   "Ancient Planetary Observations And The Validity Of Ephemeris Time", pages 220 - 221.

publication entitled "Astrology and Astronomy"[24]. In this publication are the following articles: "Why Astrology Believers Should Feel Embarrassed", "The Zodiac Isn't What It Used To Be", "Astrology Tests Show No Trends", "Scientific Tests Debunk Astrology", "Belief In The Stars Is Not A Good Sign", "Scientific Tests Fail To Support Astrology", "The Scientific Case Against Astrology", and "Some Tests of Astrology".

Astronomy is the study of the Creator's three-dimensional masterpiece in space, which leads to the determining of when the earth will have its four seasons. Astrology uses what is discovered by astronomy and then exalts the objects that were created into "gods" that are said to directly influence the affairs of men. It is important to remember the difference between the <u>science of astronomy</u> and the <u>religion of astrology</u>, and to not allow the word "Zodiac" to automatically equate to something that is evil.

6.0   The Creator And The Zodiac

The Zodiac with its twelve constellations is not a random invention of men, or of astrology, or of the devil, but is derived directly from the study of astronomy and determining why the earth has its four seasons. The

---

24   "Astrology and Astronomy". Copyright 1989. The Astronomical Society of the Pacific, 390 Ashton Ave., San Francisco, CA 94112.

Creator of the universe set in motion all that moves, and in doing this the Creator also created the Zodiac.

Perhaps the best book on this subject is "The Witness Of The Stars"[25]. This book was originally published in London over 100 years ago in 1893. In this book the author not only explains the relationship between the Creator and the Zodiac, but very effectively documents the Zodiac's greater antiquity than that of Babylonian astrology. However, the most dramatic documentation in this book is the author's itemization of the ancient names for many of the stars for each of the twelve constellations. For example on page 121:

> "The brightest star, Alpha (in the bull's eye) [of Taurus], has a Chaldee name - Al Debaran, and means the leader or governor. The star Beta (at the tip of the left horn) has an Arabic name - El Nath, meaning wounded or slain. . . . Then there is the cluster of stars known as the Pleiades. This word, which means the congregation of the judge or ruler, comes to us through the Greek Septuagint as the translation of the Hebrew 'Kimah', which means the heap or accumulation, and occurs in Job ix.9; xxxviii.31, 32, and Amos v.8."

Upon reading the names of the stars taken from many different languages the reader begins to perceive a

25   "The Witness Of The Stars", by Ethelbert W. Bullinger, D.D. Copyright 1983. Kregel Publications, Grand Rapids, MI 49501. ISBN 8254-2209-4.

definite pattern and theme for each constellation. Since the Creator has called out each star by its own name[26], the prospect that the Creator may have provided men with a message written through the names of the stars does not seem far-fetched. In doing so the Creator's own message is written in the sky and told each night as the names of each star are recited.

Perhaps the best example of how the Creator thinks about the Zodiac comes from the oldest book in the Bible, the book of Job. In reading this book the context evolves into the Creator being quoted as saying to Job:

> "Can you [Job] bind the bands of the Pleiades, or loosen the cords of Orion? Can you bring out the Zodiac [the 12 constellations, Strong's[27] number 4216] in their season; or can you guide the Bear [Arcturus] with its sons? Do you know the limits of the heavens; can you establish their rulership on the earth?"[28]

The Creator not only acknowledges the existence of the Zodiac [the twelve constellations] but very effectively

---

26   "The Interlinear Bible", Psalms 147:4: "He [the Creator] appoints the number of the stars [and] to them all [by] names He calls."

27   "Strong's Exhaustive Concordance", by James H. Strong. No Copyright Notice. Broadman Press, Nashville, Tennessee. ISBN 0-8054-1134-8.

28   "The Interlinear Bible", Job 38:33.

implies that He made them[29] and brings them out in their proper season, and that Job cannot. Also notice that the Creator knows the limits of the heavens and that He has established a "rulership" of those limits on the earth. The Hebrew word for "rulership" is Strong's number 4896, which means "jurisdiction". It does not mean "rulership" from the point of view of "giving orders", but that of "domain". The Creator was asking Job if while standing on the earth he could establish where in the sky the twelve constellations would be positioned (could Job change their domain).

The Zodiac is not something invented or mystical. The word "Zodiac" comes from the Greek word "Zodiakos" which simply means "a way or path" and has nothing to do with a zoo or animals.[30] It is derived in a very pragmatic manner as described below.

The Zodiac and its twelve sections are derived from the fact that the earth revolves around the sun once every year. This revolution around the sun is an astronomical fact, not a mystical fact. As the earth moves around the sun, the sun's heavenly position is projected back against

---

29   "The Interlinear Bible", Amos 5:8: "He who made the Pleides and Orion . . ."

30   "The Witness Of The Stars", page 15: "The word Zodiac itself is from the Greek Zodiakos, which is not from Zao, to live, but from a primitive root through the Hebrew Sodi, which in Sanscrit means a way. Its etymology has no connection with living creatures, but denotes a way, or step, and is used of the way or path in which the sun appears to move amongst the stars in the course of the year."

the backdrop of stars behind it. In this manner, each day the sun seems to move from one position in the sky to the next, until about one year later the sun has moved back to the same position it had before. This daily projection of the sun against the backdrop of stars forms an imaginary ring or circle through the stars, called the ecliptic.

The ecliptic then is the circle made by the sun's projection against the stars during the course of the year, and is also the circle that the earth follows in its own revolution around the sun. Stars above this circle are said to be "above the ecliptic", stars below this circle are said to be "below the ecliptic".

At night an observer may look up and see about one-half of the heavens at once, that is about 180 degrees. About twelve hours later an observer may see the other half of the heavens (although it is probably too bright to see any stars). If an observer held up his right hand towards the center of the night's sky and then opened wide his five fingers, he would discover that his five fingers split the sky into six sections. The six sections being those stars:

> 1) to the left of the thumb,
> 2) between the thumb and the first finger,
> 3) between the first finger and the largest finger,
> 4) between the largest finger and the third finger,
> 5) between the third finger and the smallest finger,
> 6) to the right of the smallest finger.

By sighting his largest finger upon a bright star in the center of the sky he would discover that each half of the sky had three sections. Using this mechanism, an observer could then call out to a scribe which section of the ecliptic circle a star or planet resided.

Because the earth has four seasons a year, a season can be thought of as the sun progressing through one-forth of the year's ecliptic circle. This one-forth of the year's circle may be seen as one-half of the night's sky. Since each half of the night's sky is split into three sections (using the hand's fingers spread upwards into the sky) the entire ecliptic or circle then has (four seasons times three sections) twelve sections. Thus the Zodiac has twelve sections or houses or constellations or mansions. These are just different names for the twelve divisions of the ecliptic circle.

An observer may decide to use his hand and fingers to more finely subdivide each half of the sky. In such a case the night sky would have (two halves times six finger-sections each) twelve sections in which a heavenly body may be recorded as having been seen. After including the other half of the heavens, the ecliptic circle is then subdivided into 24 sections. The night sky has twelve sections and the day sky has twelve sections. One night sky and one day sky is one turn of the earth, which is one calendar day. Call each of these sections an "hour", and what results is that each calendar day has 24 hours.

An observer may decide to use his hand and fingers to more finely subdivide each constellation into six sections. In this case the heavens would have (twelve constellations times six sections) 72 sections in which a heavenly body may be recorded as having been seen. The number 72 has more astronomical significance which will be discussed later.

The existence of a Zodiac is a fact derived from astronomy. Any mystical or religious meaning superimposed upon the Zodiac by astrologers is a matter of their own conjured-up religious belief. As pointed out above, there is profound evidence that the Zodiac and its constellations may have a message from the Creator spoken through the names that the Creator gave to the key stars in each constellation.[31] This is also a matter of religious belief.

Regardless of the reader's religious beliefs about the Zodiac, this author will now proceed to discuss the Zodiac from an astronomical point of view. It is hoped that the above discussion will enable the reader to better understand that an astronomer using the ecliptic circle and therefore using the Zodiac's existence to record sightings and observe the passage of time is not an evil religious practice.

_____

[31]   "The Interlinear Bible", Psalms 19:1-5: "The heavens declare the glory of God, and the expanse inscribes His handiwork. Day by day they pour forth speech, and night by night reveals knowledge. There is no [audible] speech, and there are no words, and their voice is not heard. [Yet] Through all the earth has gone their line and to the end of the world their words. . ."
Isaiah 40:26: "Lift up your eyes on high and look: Who has created these? Who brings out their host by number? By greatness of vigor, and might of power, He calls them all by names, not one is lacking [a name]."

7.0   Counting Time Using Circles

Because of the rotation of the earth about is own axis, the sun appears to rise and set each day. In fact most objects seen in the heavens appear to rise and set once each day. Looking out at the night sky, an observer can see about 180 degrees from horizon to horizon, or about one-half of the total heaven at once.

An observer may then draw an imaginary arc in the sky which effectively maps out the path of the sun's daily projection through the stars. This imaginary arc depicts the ecliptic through the sky. Each section of the Zodiac (each constellation along the ecliptic) would then subdivide this imaginary arc into six sections in the night's sky, or twelve sections for the whole heaven.

An observer may notice that visually the sky and these twelve subdivisions seemingly move past the western horizon and drop out of sight once each day. An observer may start to count the passage of time by watching these twelve subdivisions of the ecliptic circle slowly drop out of sight in the western horizon. The ecliptic circle, tagged by its subdivisions, move past the horizon about one constellation every two hours. Another way of describing this is to imagine that it is the horizon which is moving up the ecliptic circle. Then the time of day is determined by the distance that the horizon has moved along the circumference of the ecliptic circle.

This concept of counting time should sound very familiar. This is exactly how people tell time every day. Consider the traditional wall clock. What concept is being employed by the wall clock which allows an observer to count time? Take away all the glass and extraneous decorations which are not actually part of the clock. What is left is a simple circle which has been subdivided into equal sections, just like dividing the ecliptic circle in the heavens, which are represented by perpendicular markings on the circumference of the circle.

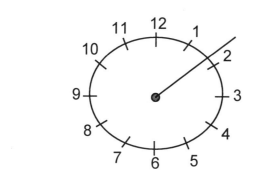

14. The Clock Is A Circle's Circumference
Divided Into Equal Sections

In accordance to the distance the "hands" move along the circumference of the clock's circle, an observer determines the time of day. The wall clock uses the same concept as the sky observer counting time by watching the horizon track along the imaginary ecliptic circle's circumference.

Both the wall clock and the ecliptic circle have been subdivided into twelve equal sections of the Zodiac.

This similarity in concept is no accident, and is a major point to be understood. "How do you count time? You count time using a circle." Time is measured by tracking along a circle's circumference which is marked with equally spaced subdivision markers. The wall clock actually has two sets of markers along the circle's circumference. One set is used to count out twelve hours and the second set of markers is used to count out 60 minutes and 60 seconds.

8.0   The Precession Of The Equinoxes

Even the most basic astronomy books make mention of the precession of the equinoxes. This astronomical phenomenon also has its roots in the fact that the earth revolves around the sun and an observer may then project the sun's image against the backdrop of stars behind it. The sun's daily path then forms an imaginary circle through the heavens called the ecliptic.

The earth follows this same imaginary ecliptic-circle as it revolves around the sun once a year. This circle in space can be thought of as a geometric plane (or a flat disk like a record). Both the sun and the earth are always spinning somewhere in this plane (on the flat record).

The earth also rotates around its own axis once each day. However, the earth's spin around its own axis is not aligned to the ecliptic plane. The axis of the earth's rotation is about 23.5 degrees slanted from the ecliptic plane. This slant is why the earth has four seasons.

All year long the earth is rotating at this 23.5 degree slant around the sun on the ecliptic plane. But the earth's line of axis always "points" in the same direction. The imaginary line of the northern axis points roughly towards the north pole star. This is why the north pole star is used in navigation in the northern hemisphere. This star can always be trusted to indicate the direction of the earth's axis of rotation.

Because the imaginary line of the earth's axis does not change direction, twice each year the slant of the axis and the earth's journey around the ecliptic plane match up so that the sun is shining equally on both the southern and northern hemispheres at the same time. These two match ups happen in just a moment in time and are called the spring and the fall equinoxes.

An observer may pinpoint the projection of the sun against the backdrop of stars behind it at the exact moment of the spring equinox. This point will lie on the ecliptic circle and may be regarded as a starting point for the year's journey around the sun. An observer may then notice that about one year later, again at the exact moment of the spring equinox, that the sun's projection against the stars behind it is not at the same point as the previous year. In fact an observer may notice that the sun slowly but steadily moves each year, so that it seems to move about one degree away every 72 years. This very slow and steady movement of the sun against the backdrop of stars behind it at the moment of the spring equinox (or fall equinox, astronomically it does not matter which equinox is used) is called the precession of the equinoxes.

This astronomical phenomenon, of the earth not getting all the way around the sun before the next equinox occurs, is caused because the spin of the earth around its axis has a slight wobble, just like a top will wobble as it spins.

The steady precession of the sun through the heavens year by year can be estimated to take about (72 years times 360 degrees) 25,920 years to traverse the entire ecliptic circle, eventually coming back the original point.

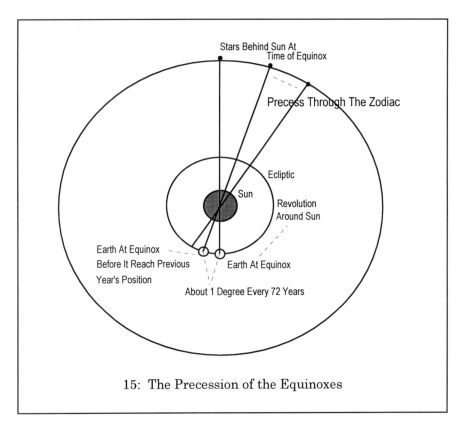

15: The Precession of the Equinoxes

To be a little more technically correct, there is a good reason why the word "estimate" is used in association with the precession taking 25,920 years. The computation of this value will remain an estimate for a long time, because the earth's wobble around its axis also has a slight wobble. That is, the wobble has a wobble. This double wobble effectively alters the exact moment of the equinoxes each year from being a constant. This double wobble, combined with the fact that the earth's revolution around the sun is not a constant, and the fact that the earth's rotation around its own axis is slowing down by a rate which also does not appear to be a constant, means that the precession cannot be computed with certainty.

Most modern reference materials on this topic will site the estimate as 25,800 years[32]. Mathematically the estimate is computed by determining that the sidereal year is about 365.25636 days long, but the next equinox will average only about 365.24220 days[33]. This results in a loss of about 0.01416 days per year. This loss is what creates the precession, the earth does not quite get back to the same point before the next equinox occurs. Using the value of 0.01416 days lost per year, then it may be computed that it will take about (365.25636 days ÷ 0.01416 days per year) 25,794.94 years to traverse the entire ecliptic circle. Thus 25,800 is a valid estimate for printing in a reference book.

9.0   Why Use 25,920 Years

While discussing ancient astronomers who observed this precession phenomenon year after year, the question about how much precision and accuracy of measurements they were able to employ becomes germane.   It is

---

[32]   "Burnham's Celestial Handbook", by Robert Burnham, Jr. Copyright 1978. Dover Publications, Inc., 31 East 2nd Street, Mineola, NY 11501. Page 55.

[33]   "Ancient Planetary Observations And The Validity Of Ephemeris Time", page 207.

manifest that the number of years to be measured being close to 25,800, and the lifetime of an astronomer being only about 70 years (probably less), meant that an astronomer could only hope to observe the sun traverse about (25,800 ÷ 70) one 368th part of the great circle in their lifetime. This is about one degree of movement per lifetime.

Of much more concern is to what precision and accuracy could ancient astronomers measure the moment of the equinox? The estimate of 25,920 is only (25,920 minus 25,800) 120 years higher than modern science estimates. This is a deviation of about (120 years ÷ 25,800 years) 0.00465, or less than one half of one percent.

Reversing the above estimation formula so that the outcome is forced to be 25,920 instead of 25,794.94 requires that the yearly loss per equinox be 0.01409 days instead of 0.01416 days. The difference in measuring the moment of equinox is only (0.01416 minus 0.01409) 0.00007 days. This is a difference in measurement of only (0.00007 days times 86,400 seconds per day) 6.048 seconds.

For the 120 year difference in the estimate to be significant the ancient astronomers would have had to be capable of measuring the moment of the equinox in units below 6.048 seconds. It seems safe to rely upon the assumption that the ancient astronomers did not measure the moment of the equinox with accuracy below 6 seconds.[34] It is therefore manifest that a deviation of only 120 years for the precession's estimate is not significant, and well within any reasonable expectations for the accuracy of ancient measurements.

For this reason using the more ancient estimate of 25,920[35] years rather than the modern estimate, when discussing how the ancients counted time by using circles, is deemed reasonable.

10.0 Astronomical Revolutions Are The Creator's Time Pieces

The science of astronomy combined with the mathematics of geometry have directly dictated our units of measure. A circle has 360 degrees, not some other number like 500. Degrees have 60 minutes each, not some other number like 100. The special numbers used in mathematics and geometry are not random or arbitrary. Rather they are derived from watching the heavens and demonstrate an order and purpose to the creation.

---

34   "Ancient Planetary Observations And The Validity Of Ephemeris Time", pages 163 - 166. Calculates from ancient astronomical records that the Greeks circa 432 BCE measured the equinoxes with an accuracy close to 0.3 days, or within (86,400 seconds per day times 0.3 days) 25,920 seconds. Thus, ancient observations of the equinox accurate to below 6 seconds is not supported by historical data.

35   "The Orion Mystery", page 189.

The existence of the heavens, the movements of the sun, moon, and planets, and the subsequent science of astronomy, all focus upon the very core of the creation. From astronomy it follows that the Creator may be using the revolutions of the heavenly objects to keep track of time. In fact it seems intuitive that the Creator, which started the objects circling one another, would use their revolutions to count the passage of time.

It is manifest that the Creator is watching time pass by observing the revolution of the earth around its own axis to measure days. It is possible that He is watching time pass by observing the revolution of the moon around the earth to measure months. Also manifest is that the Creator is watching time pass by observing the revolution of the earth around the sun to measure years.[36] Therefore, by extension, it is entirely reasonable that the Creator is also watching time pass by observing the revolution of the precession around the ecliptic circle to measure the passing of ages.

11.0   Counting Time For The Precession Of The Equinoxes

Since time is measured using the circumference of a circle, to count the 25,920 years it takes for the precession

---

[36]   "The Interlinear Bible", Genesis 1:14: "And said God, Let be luminaries in the expanse of the heavens to divide between the day and the night and let them be for signs and seasons and for days and years."

to make a full lap may be represented as the circumference of a circle with 25,920 equally spaced division markers.

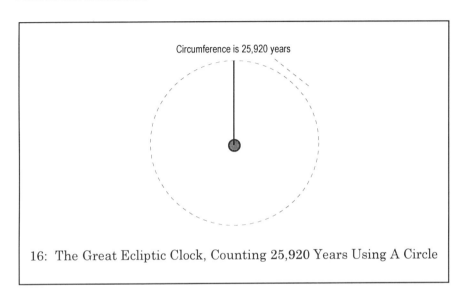

Circumference is 25,920 years

16: The Great Ecliptic Clock, Counting 25,920 Years Using A Circle

It is manifest that 25,920 subdivisions along a circle's circumference are too many to realistically mark and track. This "first clock" needs to be further divided into more manageable smaller clocks.

11.1   Dividing The Ecliptic Clock Into 12 Sections

As already explained, the ecliptic circle is subdivided into twelve equal sections. This means that each section of the ecliptic circle represents about (25,920 ÷ 12) 2,160 years. This is the number of years required for the sun to precess across one constellation of the Zodiac, and is referred to as "an age".[37]

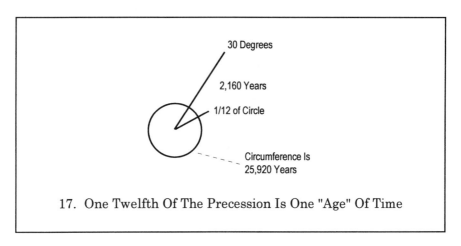

17. One Twelfth Of The Precession Is One "Age" Of Time

This number is also the diameter of the moon, which has a physical diameter of 2,160 miles[38]. The moon's diameter is not difficult to determine using simple geometry, and was known by the ancient astronomers of circa 400 BCE.[39]

37   "Serpent In The Sky", page 98.
38   "The World Almanac", 1988.   Copyright 1987.   World Almanac, 200 Park Avenue, New York, NY 10166.   ISBN 0-88687-334-7. Page 203.
39   Contrary to what has been taught, the ancient astronomers knew the earth was a sphere, its radius, circumference, and its distances from the moon and sun. With a little thought each of these values may be determined using simple tools, a little geometry, and logic.
      Watching any ship in the distant horizon coming closer reveals that the earth is curved. First the main mast can be seen, then the rest of the ship. How much the earth curves is measured using two or more tall obelisks placed in different

The unit of measure (miles) is relevant since the value 2,160 is expressed in miles and its value is what is deemed to be significant. Another unit of measure would change the value away from 2,160. Therefore, this relationship is only significant if the ancients measured in units that were related to the mile. This is precisely the

---

cities. Obelisks have been found all over the world. The length of shadow each obelisk casts on the ground will be slightly different based upon where it is on the curve of the earth. By measuring the distance between the obelisks, simple geometry will reveal the slope of the earth's curve. From this slope the radius and diameter of the earth may be estimated. Also using two or more obelisks and measuring the angle of their shadows towards the moon and the sun, creates a simple right triangle problem to which the tangent reveals the distance from the earth to the moon and sun. Timing how long it takes the moon to circle the earth will provide the moon's speed. Timing how long the moon keeps a star occulted will then provide the moon's diameter.

One of the few scrolls to survive from the library of Alexandria (Egypt) was written circa 400 BCE and describes, with diagrams, how the above procedure was actually performed by an Astronomer studying in Egypt. A similar procedure may be used for the sun, except its diameter is estimated by extending the isosceles triangle formed during a full solar eclipse.

"The Discoverers, A History of Man's Search To Know His World And Himself", page 27: A simple device used to measure the sun's shadow was discovered in Thutmose III's tomb (who lived circa 1500 BCE).

case.[40] The distance measured by a mile is (5,280 feet per mile times 12 inches per foot) 63,360 inches[41]. The British inch is nearly the same as the ancient inch of the Great Pyramid of Geza. They are so close that an ancient Egyptian astronomer would compute the distance as about 2,158 (Egyptian equivalent) miles.[42] This is less

---

[40] "The Great Pyramid, Your Personal Guide", by Peter Lemesurier. Copyright 1987. Element Books Ltd. ISBN 1-85230-016-7. The units of measure known as the English inch, foot, and mile were never exclusively the prerogative of the British. The inch, foot, Middle Eastern cubit, Greek plethrum and stadium are all related units of measure which existed two thousand years ago.

[41] "For Good Measure", by William D. Johnstone. Copyright 1975. Holt, Rinehart and Winston, New York, NY. ISBN 0-03-013946-5. Introduction: Prior to 1963 the British Imperial inch was defined to be 2.539998 centimeters. The United States inch was at that time 2.5400050 centimeters. Today, both units are defined to be exactly 2.54 centimeters. Thus, it is sometimes significant to know the year in which a measurement was taken, and by whom.

[42] "The Great Pyramid Decoded", Pages 49-51. The difference between the British Imperial inch of circa 1900 and the "Pyramid inch" is that the British inch was about (25.0265" British to 25" Pyramid) 1.00106 times shorter. Today, the modern inch is about 1.001059212 times shorter. This represents only about 67.1 modern inches of difference per mile between the two measuring units.

Measuring the distance of 2,160 miles at 63,360 modern inches per mile and then dividing by 1.001059212 yields 136,712,792 Pyramid inches. This is compared to (2,160 times 63,360) 136,857,600 modern inches, or a difference of only 144,808. This difference is about 0.1 percent. Converting this difference back to modern miles yields a distance of about (144,808 ÷ 63,360) 2.2855 miles over the span of 2,160 miles.

than the accumulated "measuring errors" that would be expected in performing such a measurement, and therefore are considered to be "the same values".

11.2 Dividing The Ecliptic Clock Into 24 Sections

A circle having 24 divisions is not an arbitrary decision. The Zodiac has twelve constellations. An observer calling out to a scribe where an object (like a planet) is positioned within one of the constellations may without effort decide to split each constellation into a "first" and a "last" half. This would give (twelve constellations times two) 24 courses to the ecliptic circle.

An observer may also decide to subdivide each half of the night's sky into six sections by simply using his hand and fingers as described earlier. In doing this an observer has effectively split the ecliptic circle into (six sections for each half of sky times two halves for night sky times two halves for the other half of the sky) 24 sections.

This results in the moon's diameter being expressed as about (2,160 minus 2.2855) 2,157.7 "Pyramid-miles". The two values 2,160 and 2,157.7 are clearly within reasonable "round off" from each other. More importantly, 0.1 percent deviance for visual measurements of an object as far away as the moon and for computing its diameter to be about 2,160 miles is well within the "measuring errors" of ancient astronomers. Thus, the difference between the two measuring systems is not significant in measuring the diameter of the moon from the vantage point of the earth. Therefore, in this case, the units may be considered to be the same.

Many times in the ancient writings of the Bible the concept of having 24 courses (sections) to complete a circle is mentioned. The Hebrew word for "course" is Strong's number 4256, which means "a section". For examples, Judges 5:20 describes "the stars from [within] their courses". In I Chronicles 27:1-28 the priests were organized into 24 courses to rotate their temple service through each year. The most plausible reason why the Zodiac has been discovered on the floor of an ancient Jewish synagogue is that they were tracking the 24 courses of temple service through the year.[43]

In Revelation 4:4 the circle around the Creator's throne is said to have 24 "seats". These 24 seats around the throne are in essence describing a circle having 24 sections. Subdividing the ecliptic circle's 25,920 years into 24 equal sections results in each section representing about (25,920 ÷ 24) 1,080 years.

In a similar fashion, every day an imaginary circle is made by the earth spinning around its own axis, and this circle is also divided into 24 sections called "hours". Most understand that an hour consists of 60 minutes. But actually the word "hour" may also be used as a title (a noun) to refer to one of the 24 sections of the circle.

[43]   "Stellar Theology and Masonic Astronomy", page 12: "Before Him were twenty-four attendants, clad in white robes and wearing golden crowns. These represented the twenty-four ancient constellations of the upper hemisphere." This quote gives evidence that the Zodiac may have originally had twenty-four sections instead of twelve.

Dividing a circle into 24 sections is a normal practice, and each section may be properly titled "an hour". Therefore, by using the word "hour" as a title (so that it no longer means exactly 60 minutes) it may be said that one "hour" (one section) of the ecliptic clock requires about 1,080 years to traverse.

Prophetically, the Bible often uses words like "hour" and "day" as titles rather than literal time spans. For example in II Peter 3:8 it states that one "day" to the Creator is like a thousand years to men. A similar statement is made in Psalms 90:4.[44] It is manifest that the word "day" is not being used to refer to a literal 24 hour period, but rather is being used as a title for a greater division of time. Time is measured using a circle. By dividing the ecliptic circle into 24 sections, the term "day" may be used as a title to refer to each section. Thus it is reasonable to project that one "day" (used as a title to refer to one section of the ecliptic circle) of the Creator's great ecliptic clock is more accurately estimated to be 1,080 years to men.

---

[44]   Other examples are Revelation 3:10, 14:7, and 17:12 which use the word "hour" as a noun. It is clear from the context that the amount of time being referred to is not intended to be interpreted as 60 minutes.

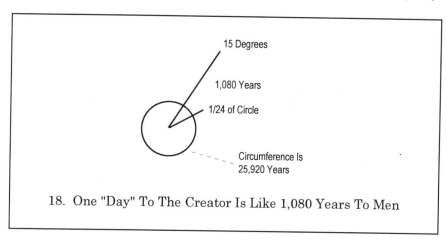

15 Degrees

1,080 Years

1/24 of Circle

Circumference Is
25,920 Years

18. One "Day" To The Creator Is Like 1,080 Years To Men

Continuing the above prophetic analogy, if 1,080 years is a "day" to the Creator, then one "hour" (one-twenty-fourth) of the Creator's "day" would be about (1,080 ÷ 24) 45 years to men. This may be significant as the terms "last hour" and "for one hour" are used several times in the context of the second advent.

This value of 45 may be significant in another prophetic relationship as well.   In Daniel 12:11-12 a prophecy specifies one time span to be 1,290 days, followed by a blessing after a second time span of 1,335 days.   The difference between these two values is 45.

A different relationship is discovered by noticing that another circle may be drawn in order to count 1,080 years. Upon forming this new clock, a circle will be drawn having its circumference split by 1,080 equally spaced markers. The Hebrew Calendar (the Hillel II calendar) splits the day into 24 hours, and each hour is split into 1,080 divisions. This means that the Hebrew Calendar's day contains (24 times 1,080) 25,920 "parts".

The ecliptic clock also has the exact same relationship in that it totals 25,920 years, it may be divided into 24 sections (like an "hour"), and each "hour" may further be subdivided into 1,080 years (like a "part"). It seems manifest that there is no accident in this relationship between the Hebrew Calendar and the precession of the equinoxes. The Hebrew Calendar's day has 25,920 parts split into 24 hours of 1,080 parts each, and the ecliptic clock has 25,920 years, with 24 courses of 1,080 years each.

11.3   Dividing The Ecliptic Clock Into 72 Sections

An observer may decide to subdivide each Zodiac constellation into another six sections each by using his hand and fingers. In doing this an observer has split the ecliptic circle into (twelve constellations times six finger-sections) 72 sections. Subdividing the 25,920 year clock into 72 equal sections results in each section representing (25,920 ÷ 72) 360 years.

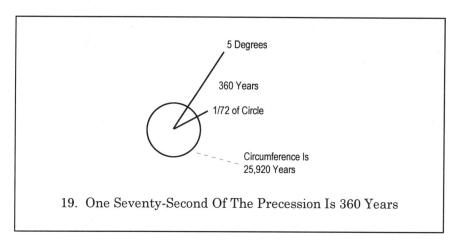

19. One Seventy-Second Of The Precession Is 360 Years

Another circle may be drawn in order to count 360 years. Upon forming this new clock to count 360 years, a circle will be drawn having its circumference split by 360 equally spaced markers. In geometry a circle then has 360 "degrees".

12.0   The Six Circles Method Of Counting Time

Time is measured or counted using the circumference of circles. The amount of time to be counted becomes the measurement for the circumference of the circle. When circles are placed within a circle, another unique geometric phenomenon occurs.

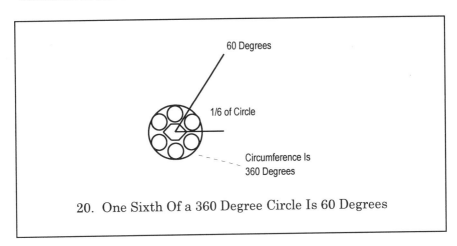

60 Degrees

1/6 of Circle

Circumference Is
360 Degrees

20. One Sixth Of a 360 Degree Circle Is 60 Degrees

Six equal size circles may be arranged inside the circumference of a larger circle. This arranging of the six inner circles to form a ring along the circumference of a larger circle is the same thing as treating a center circle as a six sided regular hexagon. The other six inner circles are placed tangent on each edge of the center hexagon. The center circle which is being treated as a hexagon is not needed after the other six inner circles are arranged.

As time is counted on the larger circle's circumference, one of the smaller inner circles is passed each time one-sixth of the total circumference of the larger circle is completed. Each smaller circle effectively represents one-sixth of the time being counted.

Starting with the smallest circle which counts for '1', then that circle will have five other circles of its same size arranged in a ring which outlines a larger circle. The larger circle will then count for '6', and it will have five other circles of its same size arranged in a ring which outlines an even larger circle. This even larger circle represents a count of 36. Repeating the expansion of the pattern out two more rings results in circles counting 216 and then 1,296. The value 1,296 is the same as six raised to the fourth power, but achieved by counting using circles instead. This sequence of 1, 6, 36, 216, and 1,296 then represents the most fundamental expansion of the Six Circles Method of counting time.

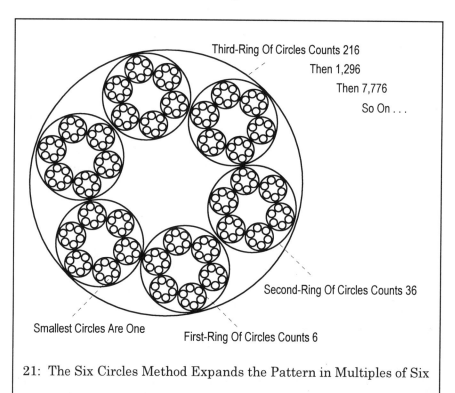

Third-Ring Of Circles Counts 216

Then 1,296

Then 7,776

So On . . .

Second-Ring Of Circles Counts 36

Smallest Circles Are One

First-Ring Of Circles Counts 6

21: The Six Circles Method Expands the Pattern in Multiples of Six

It may be noticed that the value of 1,296 (circumference of the forth-ring) is also the most fundamental unit of measure for the pyramid builders and many other cultures. For example a circle having a circumference of 1,296,000 units (the type of unit and changing the decimal-place is unimportant to the outcome) has a radius of about 206,264.8 units. The length of the Egyptian and the English cubit is 20.6264 pyramid inches (changing the decimal-place is unimportant).

Other cultures also use 1,296 as a fundamental unit of measure. For examples the Hebrew shekel weighs 129.6 grams. The English guinea weighs 129.6 grains. The Most Holy in Solomon's Temple was 1296 inches.[45]

In applying this Six Circles Method to a circle counting 360 years[46], each inner circle represents (360 years ÷ 6) 60 years. Forming a new circle to count 60 years will produce a circle having its circumference split by 60 subdivision markers.[47] The wall clock also is a circle having sixty subdivisions called minutes and / or seconds.

---

[45]   "Serpent In The Sky", page 13.

[46]   "The Discoverers, A History of Man's Search To Know His World And Himself", page 41. The Egyptians split the day into 24 hours and their circles had 360 subdivisions.

[47]   "The Prehistoric Temples of Stonehenge and Avebury", by RJC Atkinson, Professor of Archaeology, University College, Cardiff. No Copyright notice. Page 13. Stonehenge has 60 rocks arranged around it in a circle.
"Serpent In The Sky", page 97. Stonehenge has 60 stones in its outer circle.

Going the other way by expanding outward from the 360 year clock, so that the 360 year clock becomes one of six smaller circles within an even larger circle, will create a clock counting (360 years times 6 circles) 2,160 years, which is the same count as one age of the ecliptic circle.

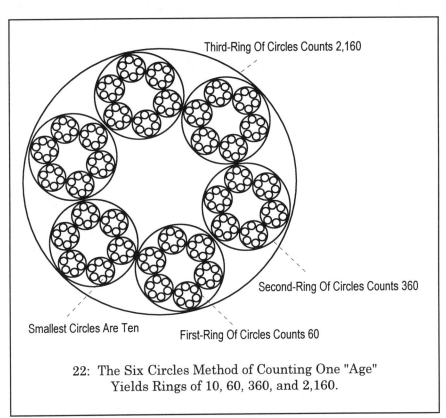

Third-Ring Of Circles Counts 2,160

Second-Ring Of Circles Counts 360

Smallest Circles Are Ten   First-Ring Of Circles Counts 60

22: The Six Circles Method of Counting One "Age"
Yields Rings of 10, 60, 360, and 2,160.

One age of time, about 2,160 years, may be counted using three clocks within a larger circle clock. The three inner clocks count in 10s, 60s, and 360s while the larger clock counts up to 2,160. It should be noticed that 10, 60, and

360, are the three most basic units of measure in our modern society. Counting is in multiples of 10, seconds and minutes are in 60s, and geometry is in 360s.

13.0   The Seventh Circle Method Of Counting Time

The Seventh Circle Method of counting time is a natural extension of the Six Circles Method. Notice that in the Six Circles Method the center, or seventh, circle is not used. The center circle is available to be used as another independent circle for additional counting.

Using the seventh circle while counting time with the Six Circles Method is called the "Seventh Circle Method" of counting time. Pictorially, the Seventh Circle Method's arrangement of seven circles looks identical to the pattern generated when using the Seven Circles Method of counting numbers. The only significant difference is that the Seven Circles Method is used to count numbers while the Seventh Circle Method is used to count time.

The Seventh Circle Method of counting time has one unique feature. As discussed previously the seventh circle is the center circle and fits perfectly in the middle of the ring of the other six circles. This inner seventh circle may contain another six smaller circles within itself, arranged in a ring around its circumference. These smaller six circles then form the exact same pattern as before, leaving room for another even smaller inner seventh circle. Then that even smaller seventh circle may have another even smaller seventh circle, and so on.

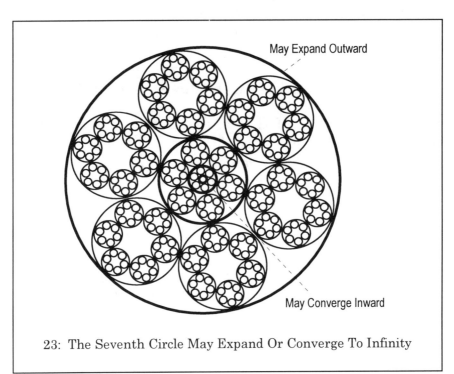

23: The Seventh Circle May Expand Or Converge To Infinity

This pattern may be extended infinitely towards smaller and smaller seventh circles, and infinitely outward towards larger and larger seventh circles. Notice how the spiraling of the seventh circle resembles a solar system's orbiting planets and the rings of electrons around an atom. The significance of using this seventh circle while counting time will be discussed later.

14.0   Summary Of Counting Using Circles

To summarize, three different methods of counting by using circles have been described:

First is the Seven Circles Method of counting numbers. This method expands the pattern while counting in rings that are progressively higher powers of seven.

Second is the Six Circles Method of counting time. This method measures the circumference of a circle by counting the six inner circles that are arranged in a ring along its circumference. Each time an inner circle is counted, one-sixth (1/6) of the circumference is measured.

Third is the Seventh Circle Method of counting time. This method is the same as the Six Circles Method, except it also counts the vacant center, or seventh, circle as an additional measure. Thus after counting all seven circles, seven-sixths (7/6) of the circumference has been measured. The pattern formed by the Seventh Circle Method of counting time may spiral inwards or outwards towards infinity by inserting smaller or larger center circles.

15.0   The Circle Methods And Prophetic Riddles

The Bible makes reference to several riddles which have been pondered long and hard by many students of prophecy. It may be possible that these riddles are difficult to understand because those who ponder them are using the wrong modern counting metaphor and not remembering that the Creator in Genesis 1:15 decreed that it would be the sun, moon, and stars that would measure the passing of time. Just as the planets and the moon circle around the sun and the earth during the passage of time, so then are circles used to measure time. Many of the Bible's prophetic riddles which focus on time may more accurately be explained from the perspective of counting time using circles.

In the following sections it will be shown how several of the Bible's prophecies and riddles are better understood by applying one of the three circle methods of counting to them. It should be understood that there are many more prophecies and riddles not discussed in this writing. The reader may enjoy applying the circle methods to some of the other prophecies and riddles in the Bible in order to determine if they too may be better understood.

15.1   The Riddle Of "The Little Scroll"

One Bible riddle is found throughout the book of Revelation. The riddle is a scroll which has seven seals, with the seventh seal having seven trumpets, with the seventh trumpet having seven plagues.

After learning about the Seventh Circle Method of counting time, this description may sound very familiar. It's exactly the same as explaining how the inner center circle is the seventh circle, which itself has a center circle, which is another seventh circle, and so on. This riddle then seems almost intuitive when looking at a circle to be used to measure time using the Seventh Circle Method, the circle being three rings deep.

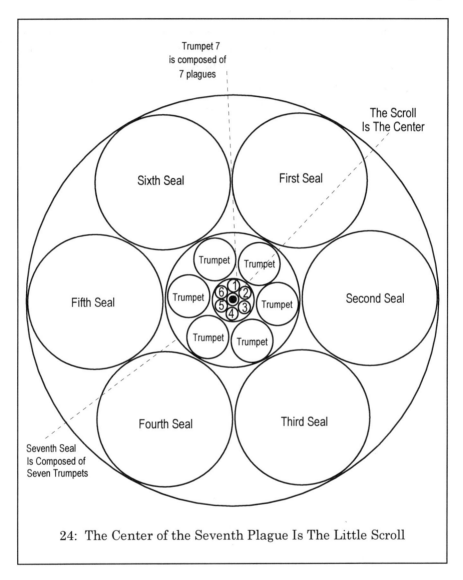

24: The Center of the Seventh Plague Is The Little Scroll

One possible implication of this interpretation of the "Little Scroll" is that each seal, each trumpet, and each plague may have a time duration associated with it. The time measured for each seal would be six times longer than for a trumpet, which would be six times longer than for a plague. The question becomes, what is the circumference of the outer-most circle? Some possibilities will be suggested in the following sections.

15.2   The Riddle Of "The 666"

In the book of Revelation 13:18 it gives the riddle about the "Mark of the Beast". This riddle specifies that there will be a mark given to men by "The Beast", that this mark is a number, that the number is the number of a man, and that the value is '666'.

When considering counting by circles, it is possible that this number is not intended to be a numerical value of '666' in the base-10 decimal system. Alternatively it may be a time indication on a circle clock. A circle clock having a pattern with three rings deep, with each ring having all six inner circles fully counted, could be specified as the value 6-circles-counted, 6-circles-counted, 6-circles-counted, or '666'. Such a specification would be a clock which happens to look exactly like "The Little Scroll" which leaves the center-most circle uncounted.

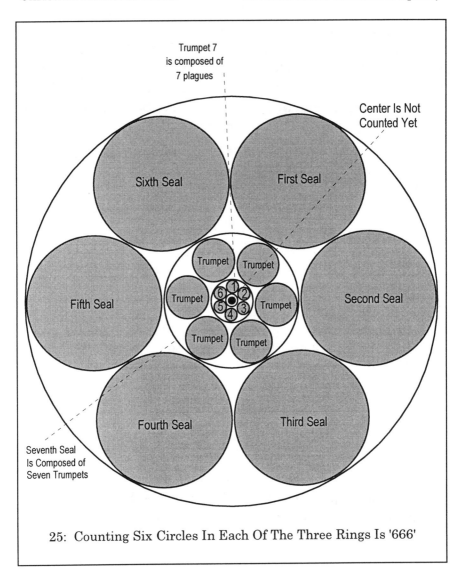

25: Counting Six Circles In Each Of The Three Rings Is '666'

If the reader would allow this alternative interpretation of this very popular riddle to be a possibility, then consider that the logical implication of this riddle (just like with "The Little Scroll") is that exact time durations are being specified with a circle clock of three rings deep.

For example, consider if the three rings deep circle clock were measuring the last age (2,160 years) before the Messiah's return. Then each of the second-rings would count (2,160 ÷ 6) 360 years, each first-ring would count (360 ÷ 6) 60 years, and each of the smallest circles would count (60 ÷ 6) 10 years each. The Seventh Circle Method specifies that the clock's inner second-ring is also counted so that the total time becomes seven-sixths larger than the clock's circumference. Using the Seventh Circle Method, the total for the circle clock would be (360 years times 7 rings) 2,520 years.

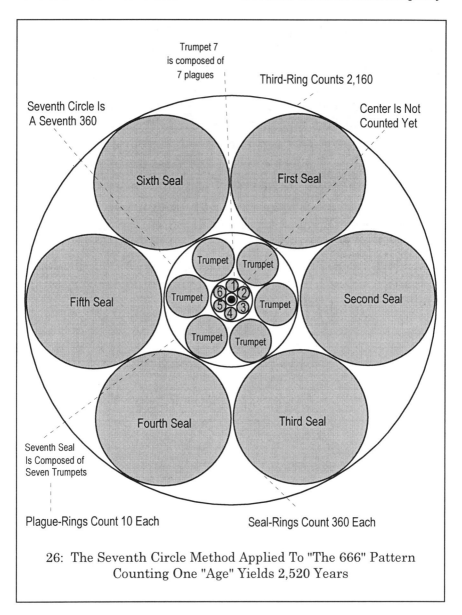

Trumpet 7
is composed of
7 plagues

Third-Ring Counts 2,160

Seventh Circle Is
A Seventh 360

Center Is Not
Counted Yet

Sixth Seal

First Seal

Trumpet

Trumpet

Fifth Seal

Trumpet

Trumpet

Second Seal

Trumpet

Trumpet

Fourth Seal

Third Seal

Seventh Seal
Is Composed of
Seven Trumpets

Plague-Rings Count 10 Each

Seal-Rings Count 360 Each

26: The Seventh Circle Method Applied To "The 666" Pattern
Counting One "Age" Yields 2,520 Years

Many readers may recognize the value of 2,520 as being a significant number in Bible prophecy. This significance will be discussed later. Since the clock is set to '666', the center-most circle is not counted yet. This means that the time value for '666' is (2,520 minus 10 for the uncounted seventh circle) 2,510 years.

Although it may prove difficult to establish beyond speculation the exact duration being prophesied by this riddle, it is still quite evident that the riddle of "The 666" appears to be much better explained or understood from the perspective of using the Seventh Circle Method of counting time and a three ring deep circle clock.

Also of interest is to discuss what will happen to the pattern of the above circle clock once the seventh and last plague is finally counted. The clock does not go from '666' to '667'. Once the last center circle is counted, the entire pattern becomes full or complete.

Because the pattern is one of circles within circles, the marking of the inner-most circle as being complete fulfills the pattern's seventh first-ring, which then immediately fulfills the seventh second-ring, which then immediately fulfills the pattern. By counting one past "The Little Scroll" pattern the time representation jumps from '666' to '777', a complete fulfillment of the pattern.

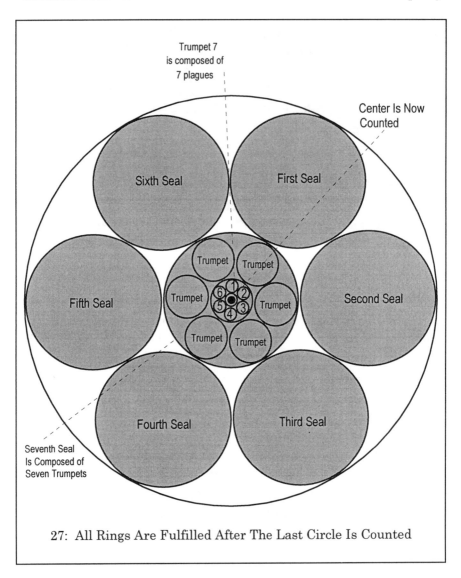

27: All Rings Are Fulfilled After The Last Circle Is Counted

Notice that if one more were now added to this fulfilled pattern, that the pattern would have to be expanded outward to the next larger fourth-ring. This would move the time representation from '777' to '1000'. Thus it may be said that the second count past "The Little Scroll" pattern forces the pattern to expand. As previously discussed, the count which forces the pattern to expand is considered to be a "new beginning". As a new beginning this second count may be celebrated in a similar manner as the 50th year Jubilee was celebrated.

15.3   The Riddle Of "The Beast"

In the book of Revelation 17:8 and 11 it gives the riddle about "The Beast" which <u>was</u>, and <u>is not</u>, and <u>notwithstanding it is</u>, and <u>is an eighth</u>, and <u>is of the seven</u>. This riddle seems confusing even when read slowly. However when considering the Seven Circles Method of counting numbers, this riddle is easily understood.

The center circle is not really there, but it is implied by the other six circles which are arranged in a ring. Yet at the same time the center circle is always there and available. The center circle is of the seven (it is the same size as the other six inner circles) and yet at the same time may be numbered as the eighth circle by allowing the larger outer implied circle to be counted as being the seventh instead. Thus the center circle is "of the seven" and is "an eighth" at the same time.

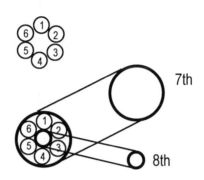

28: The Center Circle "Is An Eighth" Circle, and also
"Is Of The (Smaller) Seven" Circles

During the counting process the center circle is used to count the value seven after the other six circles have counted from one through six. So therefore if the count is beyond seven, the center circle "was" already used, and so may be expressed as being already past tense, "it was".

7   

29: The Center Circle "Was" Used for Counting the Number Seven

At the count of 8 the pattern expands to form a new center circle. This new and larger center circle is not used during the counting between 8 and 42. By not being used, the center circle "is not" part of the counting. At exactly the same time the new center circle is also "coming" in the count. It will be used once again. From this perspective the seventh circle exists, is not being used, and "notwithstanding it is" there and ready.

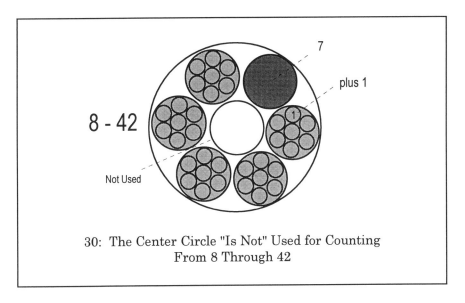

30: The Center Circle "Is Not" Used for Counting
From 8 Through 42

When the counting goes beyond 42 and reaches 43, the seventh circle is used once again.

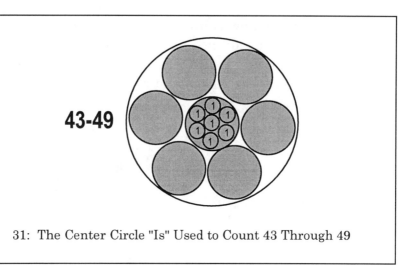

31: The Center Circle "Is" Used to Count 43 Through 49

Thus the Seventh Circle Method of counting numbers provides a better understanding of this riddle. The seventh circle meets all of the riddle's twists. The seventh circle <u>was</u>, and <u>is not</u>, and <u>notwithstanding it is</u>, and <u>is an eighth</u>, and <u>is of the seven</u>. Notice that "The Beast" riddle "breaks apart" at the count of 50. At 50 the pattern would need to expand to a larger pattern.

Also of interest is to only consider the innermost center circle, regardless of the size of the pattern. This perspective may be appropriate in that "The Little Scroll" pattern has the exact center circle left uncounted. In only stating what happens to the absolute exact center circle, it may be said that the innermost circle, "was" used in the count of 7, "was not" used in the count of 8 through 48, and "is" to be used to count exactly 49. If the count has not reached 49, then the innermost circle "is" coming while the counting process is anywhere between 8 and 48.

15.4   The Riddle Of "The Lord God Almighty"

In the book of Revelation 4:8 a riddle is given about the "Lord God Almighty". It states that He is the one who <u>was</u>, and <u>is</u>, and <u>is coming</u>. This riddle is also better understood by using the Seven Circles Method of counting numbers.

In counting from one to seven, the seventh circle is used. When stating this in the past tense it may be said that the seventh circle "was" used to count the value seven.

7

32: The Seventh Circle "Was" Used for Counting the Number Seven

Upon the count of eight the pattern is expanded forming a new center circle. During the count from 8 onto 42, nothing happens with the seventh circle, it is not used.

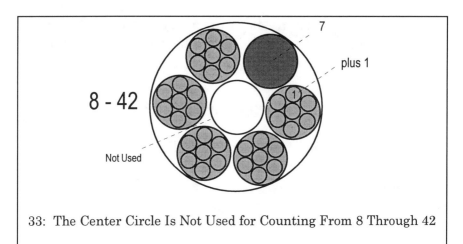

33: The Center Circle Is Not Used for Counting From 8 Through 42

When the counting progresses past 42, the seventh circle is once again used. It is then used from 43 to 48.

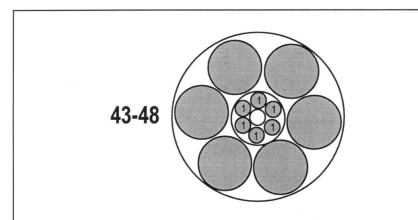

34. The Seventh Circle "Is" Used For Counting Between 43 and 48

When the counting goes past 48 and reaches exactly 49, the very innermost seventh circle will be used. Therefore, in this riddle the count has not reached 49 yet. The innermost seventh circle "is still coming" in the counting process.

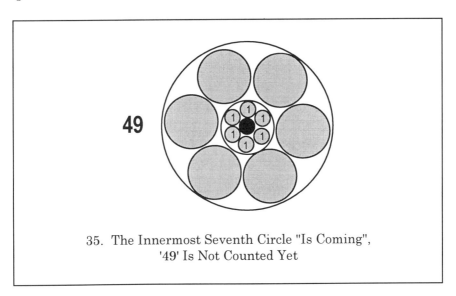

35. The Innermost Seventh Circle "Is Coming",
'49' Is Not Counted Yet

Consider looking at both "The Beast" and the "Lord God Almighty" riddles at the same time. Combining the two riddles it may be observed that both riddles and both counts are valid together. That is, combining both riddles means that whomever is doing the counting has already counted 1 through 42, is now counting somewhere between 43 and 48, but has not reached the count of 49 yet.

15.5 The Riddle Of "The Four Living Creatures"

In the book of Revelation 4:4-8 a riddle is given about the throne of the Creator. In the midst of the throne and around the throne are "four living creatures". Also mentioned around the throne are the seats for 24 elders. The 24 elders will be discussed later.

In the prophetic account each of the four living[48] creatures are described. They appear like a lion, an eagle, a man, and a young bullock. In Ezekiel chapter one and ten a similar description is given. Upon comparing these creatures to the constellations of the Zodiac an interesting correlation is discovered. These four creatures match the four consecutive constellations of Leo, Cancer, Gemini, and Taurus.[49]

---

[48]   The Bible sometimes uses the term "living" to refer to the object being in motion. It does not always mean that the object is alive or has life. For example in John 4:10 is the expression "living water". In English the expression is "running water". In I Peter 2:4 is the expression "living stone". In English the expression is "rolling stone". The objects are just moving, not alive. The four living creatures around the throne are in motion.

[49]   "Stellar Theology and Masonic Astronomy", subtitle "The Lion, The Eagle, The Ox, and The Man", pages 92 - 93: "In all ancient astrological projections of the heavens, the four great angles of the zodiac, where the celestial gods were seated, were marked by the figures of the lion, the eagle, the ox, and the man . . ."

The reader is provided with the above alternative understanding of the symbolism for the four living creatures. This alternative understanding effectively places each creature at one of the four "corners" of the ecliptic circle to

To most readers the relationship of the lion to Leo, and of the bullock to Taurus, will not be seriously questioned. However many readers will seriously question how the eagle and the man match "a crab" and the "twins". The answer to this concern is not a short one. It starts by explaining that the modern astrologers provide their list of the signs of the Zodiac as they were depicted by the first century BCE Babylonian and Greek astrologers. By doing this they are hiding the fact that in other cultures the Zodiac's constellations have other names, and are represented by other symbols, and are depicted differently in their Zodiac pictures. The short answer is that "the crab" and "the twins" are "our" symbols for these constellations. Historically they have been depicted differently.

15.5.1   The Bible And "The Eagle"

In the Bible the Greek word translated as "eagle" is Strong's number 105, and generally means "eagle". However, this is a general translation and is not specific

---

match the two solstices and the two equinoxes. Thus the four creatures surround the full circle of the ecliptic.

However, it is important to notice that the above interpretation of the four creatures is an "astrological" depiction based upon astrology, not astronomy. This author will provide evidence that these four creatures are better represented astronomically within the four consecutive constellations of Leo, Cancer, Gemini, and Taurus, which is only one third of the ecliptic circle.

to any one of the many varieties of hawk to which the eagle belongs.

For example, other hawks are the falcon, the owl, and the vulture. The point is that the bird being described as an "eagle" could be a traditional looking Roman style eagle, or an Egyptian falcon, or an African vulture, or any one of a number of other varieties of hawk, and still be translated as "eagle". This ambiguity is pointed out in the "Thayer Greek-English Lexicon".[50] For this reason the words "hawk", "falcon", and "vulture" are not found in the King James version of the New Testament writings. However any one of these different varieties of hawk may nevertheless be what was meant whenever the word "eagle" is used in the New Testament.

One of the reasons why the traditional Roman eagle is considered a valid translation in the context of Revelation 4:4 is that it is presumed that the description is intended to be the same as was given by Ezekiel. For example in Ezekiel 1:10 the word "eagle" is also used, but translated from a Hebrew word.

In the Hebrew the word translated as "eagle" is Strong's number 5405, which means "to lacerate, an eagle or any other large bird of prey". The Hebrew language has two other words that also could have been used by the writer. These two Hebrew words are Strong's number 5322,

50   "Thayer Greek-English Lexicon", by Joseph Henry Thayer. Copyright 1977. Baker Book House, Grand Rapids, MI. ISBN 0-8010-8872-0. Page 13.

which means "a flower" or "a hawk", and number 8464 which means "a night hawk (an owl)". Therefore the only certainty which may be derived from Ezekiel's description and choice of word is that the animal is a large bird of prey and is not a night hawk (an owl). Also, it is probably not an African style vulture as Ezekiel did not use the term for vulture (#5322) when he could have. This leaves the Roman type of eagle and the Egyptian falcon as example candidates to represent the type of hawk being described by Ezekiel.

15.5.2 The Zodiac And "The Eagle"

Pictures depicting the constellations of the Zodiac have been unearthed around the world. Nearly every culture that has existed knew about, used, and had words in their own language which described the Zodiac, its symbols, its constellations, and the names of the stars within each constellation.

Recently an ancient Jewish synagogue was unearthed near Ephesus in Asia Minor. Very prominently depicted on the floor of this synagogue is a rather large picture of the Zodiac. The reader may immediately wonder what the Zodiac has to do with a Jewish Synagogue? Of special note is that the symbol for the constellation of Cancer is not a crab, but is a circle of leaves and vine, in the form of a wreath. A wreath, like a ring, is an encircling symbol.

One of the most well known Zodiac pictures discovered is from the Temple of Denderah (Egypt). This temple was constructed by the Ptolemy kings in the first century BCE upon the site of an earlier temple.[51]   One of the more peculiar aspects about this depiction of the Zodiac is that "the crab" is drawn in the wrong spot. Most references to this Zodiac's depiction note that the constellation of Cancer is obviously off-center from where it should be, which is on the ecliptic like the other eleven constellations. What is really amazing is that the authors studying the Denderah Zodiac never even question that "the crab" may not be the correct symbol for Cancer to the ancient Egyptians. Instead they chose to excuse the fact that the crab is drawn in the wrong spot as being an error on the ancient artist.

However, the much more obvious conclusion is that the symbol that was drawn by the artist at the exact ecliptic location of Cancer was indeed drawn as their recognized symbol for Cancer. The symbol drawn is a man with a falcon's head (a hawk or eagles head) holding a rod, and is most probably that of the Egyptian religion's god, Sokar[52]. The rod itself is a symbol for a male deity. Sokar was the god who protected the souls of the dead in the Duat. The crab symbol drawn in this Zodiac clearly

---

51   "Serpent In The Sky", pages 100 - 101.

52   "The Orion Mystery": Sokar is the most probable choice, as he best fits the overall Egyptian mythology involving the Duat, Orion and the Milky Way, page 117 - 120. However, it could also be the Egyptian god Horus which was also depicted as a man with a falcon's head, page 20 and 204-207.

represents one of the other decans[53], and is most probably representing the decan Ursa Major[54].

The best evidence for what the Egyptian symbolism was for the constellation of Cancer is that the name given to this constellation in their own language was not "Cancer" or "Crab", but was "Klaria", a word meaning "Cattlefolds".[55] As protector or keeper of the souls of the dead, Sokar was like a shepherd of a "holding pin", much like a keeper of a cattlefold. A shepherd's duty is to protect and nourish the flock by providing them with protection. The best protection is to place a flock into a ringed corral or other type of encirclement. Thus Sokar as the keeper of the "Cattlefolds" establishes a cohesive symbolism for this constellation within the Egyptian mythology.

By examining the ancient names of the stars within the constellation of Cancer, a very clear theme emerges which clearly establishes the original symbolism of the constellation given in antiquity. As examples: the two stars in the middle are called the "two asses (donkeys)". One of the nebulous clouds is named "Praesepe", meaning

---

53   Each of the twelve constellations of the Zodiac is comprised of three "rows" of constellations called decans. The word "decan" is just another term for the words section, or division. Thus there are 36 decans along the ecliptic. Each decan has its own symbol and occupies specific stars.

54   "The Orion Mystery", page 206.

55   "God's Voice In The Stars", by Kenneth C. Fleming. Copyright 1981. Loizeaux Brothers, Inc., Neptune, New Jersey. Page 123-133.

"The Manger or A Multitude, Offspring". The Arabs called the constellation "Alsartan" and the Syriac language called it "Sartano", which both mean "Who Holds or Binds". The Hebrews called the constellation "Ausar", which means "To Bind or To Harness or To Hold or To Keep" and is used in the book of Genesis 49:11. The brightest star is called "Tegmine", meaning "Holding". Other stars have names which mean "Sheltering or Hiding Place", "Assembled Thousands", "The Kids or The Lambs", and "Multitude".[56] The Greeks called this constellation "Karkinos", which means "Holding or Encircling". The Akkadian name for it was "Sukulna", "The Seizer or The Possessor of Seed". The other two decans associated with this constellation have very similar names to these stars as well.[57]

The pattern or theme which emerges is that some star names symbolize that there is an encirclement, other star names symbolize what is inside of the encirclement, and other star names symbolize the holding or keeping of the encirclement. Consider that history has preserved the names which describe "Holding", "Binding", "Harnessing", "Keeping", "Seizing", and "Encircling". These are verbs which denote determined grasping of whatever is being held within the encirclement. It is manifest that a person or an animal can grasp or hold something for two reasons, either to attack it or to protect it.

---

56   "God's Voice In The Stars", pages 125-126.
57   "The Witness Of The Stars", pages 147 - 148.

It seems reasonably safe from the above to state that this constellation is representing the symbolism of holding or binding something for the purpose of protecting it within an encirclement. The reader may visualize why a crab may be chosen to represent this concept. The crab's claws both grasp and provide an encircling posture. To make a contrast, consider that a chicken would not make an adequate symbol. A chicken does not grasp or bind her chicks, but only encircles them with the wings to protect them. There are other animals which may be chosen to represent this constellation's symbolism.

The eagle (Roman style eagle or Egyptian falcon) is another animal that may be chosen. It may be difficult to visualize an eagle under stress trying to protect her chicks, but consider that the eagle is just a majestic looking hawk. Being a hawk the eagle has claws which grasp, hold, or bind, and wings which even in flight give an encircling posture.

Consider how the United States and most other nations around the world use the eagle as a symbol. The eagle is usually found as a symbol of "national defense", but is used in other contexts as well. However, few depictions show the eagle actually attacking.

Upon giving the prevalence of the eagle-symbol some thought, one may realize that in fact the symbol of the eagle is found "everywhere". Most depictions show the eagle grasping something, such as arrows and olive branches, with its wings spread in an encircling motion. It is not hard to perceive what is being portrayed by these images. Men and nations have always used the eagle as a symbol for grasping hold of the implements for defense, and to protect with an encircling motion.

The eagle is an animal which almost universally represents the symbolism described by the names of the stars in the constellation of Cancer. By considering all of the evidence, it is not unreasonable that the eagle was the symbol of this constellation in ancient times. Even so, notice that as late in history as the first century BCE the Egyptians still symbolized this constellation as a man with a falcon's (eagle's) head.

15.5.3   The Zodiac And "The Man"

In modern times the constellation of Gemini is typically depicted as "two twins", sometimes as two baby boys, and sometimes as two men. However, the depiction of the constellation of Gemini as a man and a woman was prevalent in the Middle Ages.[58]

The Zodiac depiction from the temple of Denderah (circa first century BCE) in Egypt portrays this constellation as being a man and a woman joined together by holding hands. Gender is evident from the garments drawn, the male has a belt, the female does not.[59] The Egyptians named this constellation "Clusus" or "Claustrum Hor", which means "The Place of Him Who Cometh". The

---

58   "The Sky, Mystery, Magic, and Myth", page 40.
59   "The Orion Mystery", page 207.

Coptic name is "Pi-Mahi", which means "The United". Most of the other stars have names in different languages which are variations to the themes of "He Comes" and "United".[60]

In Ezekiel 1:10 where the face of a "man" is described, the Hebrew word is Strong's number 120 which means "a human being, mankind". In Revelation 4:7 the Greek word for "man" is Strong's number 444, which means "man-faced" ("Anthropos"). This cross-reference makes it manifest that these scriptures are not attempting to depict the sex of the face of the creature being described, but are generically describing the face of a human being.

The constellation of Gemini being portrayed as a man and a woman and being called "united" represents mankind as a married couple. A man and woman united and becoming the same as one flesh is a principle dating back to the creation of Adam and Eve. As two people being united as one flesh, a singular image may be used, which is essentially mankind. The ancient names for this constellation are in the masculine singular tense, for examples "He comes" and "Him who comes". From the perspective of social history, mankind is essentially a man and a woman mated together to form a single unit. Portraying this constellation's symbolism as a human's face to represent both a man and a woman is highly consistent with the evidence of ancient history.

60　　"The Witness Of The Stars", pages 137 - 138.

15.5.4 The Four Ages Of The Creator's Plan

From the above research it is deemed reasonable to speculate that the four creatures around the throne are a reference to the Zodiac constellations of Leo, Cancer, Gemini, and Taurus. These four constellations are in sequence with each other, that is each lies next to the other along the ecliptic.

It takes the sun approximately 2,160 years to precess each one of the four constellations. Four constellations therefore requires about (2,160 x 4) 8,640 years to precess. By referencing four sequential constellations and specifying that they lie "around the throne", the writer is depicting the same image as a circle around the throne being subdivided into four sections. This then is a circle clock measuring four ages or 8,640 years along its circumference. Is it possible that the Creator has allotted four ages to complete a plan?

Nearly all Bible chronologies estimate that Adam and Eve stood in the Garden of Eden around the year 4005 BCE. Adding plus or minus 50 years to this estimate would capture nearly all other estimates.

Many readers will have at their disposal one of the many astronomy programs now available on the home computer.[61] Using one of these programs, setting the

---

61   For example this author uses a commercially available IBM
        PC compatible program called: "Interactive Astronomy and
        Historical Calendars Reconstruction", available through Z2

date to around 4000 BCE, and ensuring that the program is set up to adjust for the precession of the equinoxes, find the date for the astronomical summer solstice[62] when the sun is at right ascension of six hours, exactly. For example try Julian Day number 260,629 which is Julian calendar date July 25, 4000 BCE.

It may then be noticed that on that day of the astronomical summer solstice the sun lies in-between the constellations of Virgo and Leo. To be a little more accurate, the sun lies between Beta Virgo and Beta Leo. This means that in the time frame of Adam and Eve the precession, as viewed from the perspective of the summer solstice, was leaving one age, Virgo, and moving into a new age, Leo. The constellation of Leo is the first of the four constellations that surround the throne as described in the book of Revelation.

As the astronomy program allows the years to go by, the astronomical summer solstice will by definition always keep the sun at the right ascension of exactly 6 hours. But the stars, because of the precession of the equinoxes, will shift very slowly so that the sun fully enters the

---

Computer Solutions, 439 Molino Avenue, Sunnyvale, CA 94086.

[62] The reasons for using the summer solstice rather than one of the equinoxes are: 1) using any one of the equinoxes or solstices to watch the precession is a valid choice, and 2) many ancient calendars were based upon the summer solstice, rather than upon the spring equinox as is the modern Gregorian calendar. For example the Greek Olympiad was based upon the summer solstice.

"front" portion of the constellation of Leo. As additional years go by the precession moves the sun further away from Virgo, while moving the sun further into and later all the way through Leo.

Letting the program move about 2,160 years later it may be noticed that the sun is leaving Leo and begins to enter into the second constellation of Cancer. About the time of Jesus, the sun is leaving Cancer and entering into Gemini. Currently, in 1996, the sun is leaving Gemini and entering into Taurus. Taurus is the fourth and last constellation around the throne.

From this exercise it may be noticed that the sun's precession is still within the very same "age" as was Jesus when He gave His prophecies about the end of the age. That is, we are still within the very same 2,160 years since Jesus spoke those words. The precession is only now beginning to leave Gemini and move into Taurus.

Today, many who study Bible prophecy predict that Jesus the Messiah will return, for the final battle and resurrection of the dead into eternal life, within the next few years. Such predictions may turn out to be completely accurate, based upon the observation that "time" is now at the end of an age.

Although totally obscured when reading the King James version of the scriptures, Jesus and the apostles consistently used the Greek word "aion" (Strong's number 165) when discussing the long sought for event of the second advent. The Greek word "aion" means "age". For example:

- In Matthew 24:3 the apostles ask Jesus: "tell us of your coming and of the end of the age".

- In Matthew 13:39 Jesus is quoted as saying: "and the harvest is at the end of the age".

- In Mark 10:30 Jesus is quoted as saying: "in the age coming [he will receive] eternal life."

In these examples, it may be noticed that Jesus and others purposefully distinguished between the end of the age which was then, Gemini, and the age which was to come, Taurus.

- In Ephesians 2:7 it states that: "He [the Creator] might show in the coming ages the exceeding great riches of His grace in kindness towards us in Christ Jesus".

The Biblical use of the term "age" may be more astronomically based than many have supposed.

It is not a coincidence that the astronomical movements of the sun, earth and stars have just now reached the point of leaving one age (Gemini) and getting close to entering the last of the four ages (Taurus) in the Creator's plan. In Revelation 20:4 it states that after the return of Jesus as the Messiah, that Jesus will be granted His own reign for about 1,000 years.   Assuming that Jesus returns very shortly, His 1,000 year reign will move time forward to about half way through the next age of Taurus. According to the ecliptic clock, this approximate 1,000 year reign will occur within the seventh course ("day") since Adam and Eve, and represents the "Great Sabbath Rest" as described in Hebrews 4:9. The "millennium" will actually be a Sabbath "Days" rest with the Messiah.

In I Corinthians 15:24 it states that after the reign of Jesus the Messiah, He will then turn His kingdom over to the Creator.   This event then moves human history towards the completion of the fourth age since creation, having everything finally being completely restored.   In this grand event the eighth course since creation is counted, wherein the circle counting pattern is expanded into a new larger pattern, and mankind takes a new beginning as time enters into all of the ages of eternity yet to come.

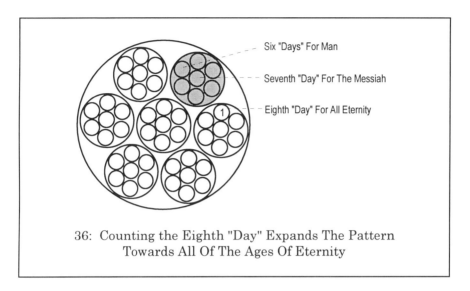

36: Counting the Eighth "Day" Expands The Pattern
Towards All Of The Ages Of Eternity

The final lesson may be that the Creator has allotted six "days", of about 1,080 years each, for mankind to "do their own works of good and evil". Then He has allotted one "day" for the reign of His son the Messiah to occur during the seventh "day" of the promised Sabbath rest. Then on the eighth "day" the (imaginary) circle counting pattern will be forced to expand, making the eighth "day" a new beginning leading into all of the ages of eternity.

The Creator is not bound by time. Therefore it should not be a tremendous stretch to consider that He may have measured out a plan which spans in the neighborhood of 8,640 years. To the Creator, this is just one-third of a turn on the ecliptic circle. The earth has four seasons which is also one-third of its revolution around the sun. All of human history may become just one season in the eyes of the Creator.

Even so, one fact remains a certainty. According to the great astronomical clock of the ecliptic circle, which the Creator has made, time is currently moving out of one age and into another. We are literally at the end of the age.

15.5.5 The Throne And "The 24 Elders"

In Revelation 4:4 it is said that 24 seats are also placed around the throne. If the throne is surrounded by four ages, then these four ages are to be subdivided into 24 sections. Mathematically this would mean that each of the 24 seats represents about (8,640 ÷ 24) 360 years. Each elder would then represent or be given a span of about 360 years.

Many readers may recognize the number 360 as a significant value often used while discussing Bible prophecy. Many use a 360 day long year (instead of the astronomical tropical year of 365.2422 days per year) during their computations of some prophetic timelines.[63]

Alternatively, as described earlier, dividing the full ecliptic circle into 24 sections results in (25,920 ÷ 24) 1,080 years, which is one half of an age per elder's seat.

---

63   "The Witness Of The Stars", pages 177 - 189, especially 180.
        There are numerous references which may be listed. This one
        is chosen due to the book's greater age having been written in
        1893.

16.0   The Six Circles Method And The Four Ages

In forming the pattern to count the time required for the sun to precess across four constellations of the ecliptic circle, or four ages, a clock is drawn with its circumference being about (25,920 ÷ 4) 8,640 years. Employing the Six Circles Method of counting time, each of its second-rings would have circumferences of (8,640 ÷ 6) 1,440 years each.

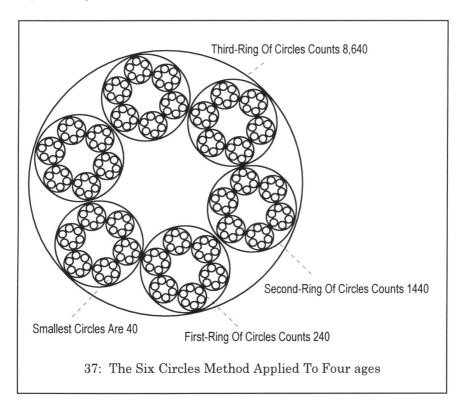

Third-Ring Of Circles Counts 8,640

Second-Ring Of Circles Counts 1440

Smallest Circles Are 40

First-Ring Of Circles Counts 240

37: The Six Circles Method Applied To Four ages

The value 1,440 is the number of seconds within each division of the day as defined by the Babylonians, Ptolemy (circa 142 CE) and the Hindus.[64] Astronomers from these regions sometimes split the day into 60 divisions instead of 24. Each division then had (86,400 seconds per day ÷ 60) 1,440 seconds each. There are three other points about the number 1,440 to be noticed:

1) Making another clock to count 1,440 years will form a pattern having six smaller inner circles of (1,440 ÷ 6) 240 years each. The value 240 is five factorial times two, (5! * 2).

2) The value 1,440 is itself six factorial times two, (6! * 2).

3) Counting the same clock but by using the seventh circle method (by counting the implied circle in the middle of the other six) results in a value of (1,440 years times 7 circles) 10,080 years. The value 10,080 is seven factorial times two, (7! * 2).

Upon employing the Seven Circles Method with the same clock counting 8,640 yields rings of (7/6 times 240) 280, (7/6 times 1,440) 1,680, and (7/6 times 8,640) 10,080.

---

64   "The Discoverers, A History of Man's Search To Know His World And Himself", page 42. The Babylonians and Ptolemy divided the day into 60 units.
"Serpent In The Sky", page 46. The Hindus divided the day into 60 units.

Also, the value 8,640 times 10 is the number of seconds in a solar day of the earth, that is (24 hours times 60 minutes times 60 seconds) 86,400 seconds. This fact gives evidence that our most fundamental unit of measuring time, the second, is directly tied to both the ecliptic precession and to the four ages.

17.0   The Seventh Circle Method And "The 2,550"

In forming the pattern to count the time required for the sun to precess across one constellation of the ecliptic circle, or one age, a clock is drawn with its circumference being (25,920 ÷ 12) 2,160 years. Employing the Seventh Circle Method of counting time, each of its second-rings would have circumferences of (2,160 ÷ 6) 360 years each.

Notice that this is the exact same pattern as previously explained for the riddles of the "Little Scroll" and "The 666".

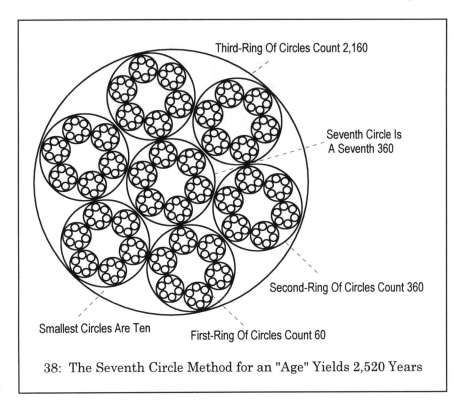

38: The Seventh Circle Method for an "Age" Yields 2,520 Years

By employing the Seventh Circle Method of counting time, the implied seventh inner circle, representing an additional 360 years, is counted in addition to the other six circles. This results in the value of (360 years per circle times 7 circles) 2,520 years.

Many readers will recognize the significance and correlation of the term "seven times" and the value 2,520. Both are referenced prophetically in the Bible. For example: In Leviticus 26:18, 21, and 24 it describes how God (in Hebrew "YHVH") will punish Israel "seven times more" for their sins. Many have speculated that the value 2,520 is the number of years prophetically pronounced upon the kingdom of Babylon in Daniel 5:25-27. The numerical value of the words which "YHVH" wrote on the wall during Belshazzar's feast adds up to 2,520.

18.0   The Seventh Circle Method And "The 1,260"

In forming the pattern to count the time required for the sun to precess across one course (one twenty-fourth) of the ecliptic circle, or one "day"[65] unto the Creator, a clock is drawn with its circumference being (25,920 ÷ 24) 1,080 years. Each of its second rings would have circumferences of (1,080 ÷ 6) 180 years each.

---

65   The word "day" is being used as a title (or noun) to refer to a single one-twenty-fourth section of the ecliptic circle.

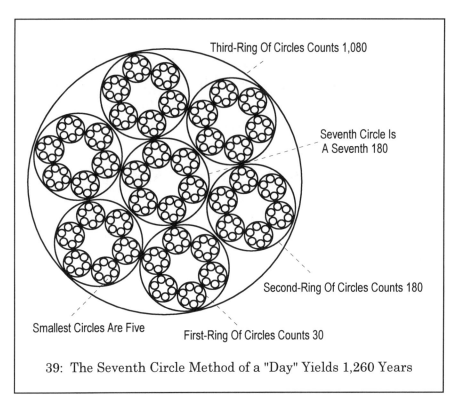

Third-Ring Of Circles Counts 1,080

Seventh Circle Is
A Seventh 180

Second-Ring Of Circles Counts 180

Smallest Circles Are Five

First-Ring Of Circles Counts 30

39: The Seventh Circle Method of a "Day" Yields 1,260 Years

By employing the Seventh Circle Method of counting
time, the implied seventh inner circle, representing 180
years, is counted after the other six circles. This results
in the value of (180 years per circle times 7 circles) 1,260
years. Many readers may recognize the significance of
the value 1,260 as it is used in Revelation 11:3 and 12:6
as prophetic timelines for the two witnesses of God and
for the Christian church.

19.0 Conclusion

Everything a person knows about the world around them is only derived from what they have been taught by others. It is manifest that if there is something they have not been taught then they have no way of knowing about its absence.

For instance, until reading about counting time using an alternative method from what is taught as modern arithmetic, that is counting with circles, the reader may not have had any idea of viewing the Bible's timelines, prophecies, and riddles from the point of view of circles within circles. Perhaps what is not taught may be more damaging than what is taught. For an untruth can only be believed if the truth is either not taught or poorly presented.

It is not within the scope of this writing to engage in speculation about specific timelines for each prophetic riddle. For now it is sufficient that the reader may understand that there is a mathematical relationship between the created heavens and the prophetic timelines in the Bible. Presenting a few examples of possible timelines may serve as a stimulus for the reader to find other possibilities. It is fully anticipated that many readers will progress from this understanding into searching for and finding significant clues which will allow for the assigning of less speculative values to the circumferences of each prophetic circle clock in the Bible.

This book has documented some of the evidence describing the relationship between the movements in the heavens and the prophetic riddles of the Bible. By presenting this relationship, the reader is provided additional evidence that the universe is not randomly moving; that there is organization to the movements in the heavens, that there is a Creator; that the Creator has specified prophetic riddles recorded in the Bible; and that these riddles may be understood by studying the Creator's three dimensional masterpiece called the universe, and by knowing how to count time using circles.

About The Author, Wayne L. Atchison

Graduate of Chico State University in 1974, Bachelor of Science degree in Computer Science.

Current occupation is a Senior Software Engineering Specialist.

Served six years on the Board of Directors for The Biblical Church of God.

Ordained an Elder in the Church of God, Bonny Doon Christian Fellowship, in 1990.

Engaged in Biblical, historical, and ancient astronomical research for 23 years.

Under the title of "Christian Technical Notes", have authored numerous articles relating to Biblical topics, especially using astronomy to date ancient records and thereby reconstruct ancient calendars and chronologies.

Featured speaker giving sermons and Bible studies by invitation to various church congregations in northern California and central Oregon.

Developed computer software called: "Interactive Astronomy with Historical Calendar Reconstruction's", which is commercially available. Developed four other commercially available software products.

Husband and father of three boys, 20, 17, and 7.